Carol Moseley-Braun

AFRICAN-AMERICAN LEADERS

Carol Moseley-Braun

Henry Louis Gates, Jr.

Benjamin Hooks

Eleanor Holmes Norton

Condoleezza Rice

Cornel West

AFRICAN-AMERICAN LEADERS

Carol Moseley-Braun

Wayne D'Orio

CHELSEA HOUSE
PUBLISHERS
A Haights Cross Communications Company
Philadelphia

CHELSEA HOUSE PUBLISHERS
VP, NEW PRODUCT DEVELOPMENT Sally Cheney
DIRECTOR OF PRODUCTION Kim Shinners
CREATIVE MANAGER Takeshi Takahashi
MANUFACTURING MANAGER Diann Grasse

Staff for CAROL MOSELEY-BRAUN
EDITOR Sally Cheney
EDITORIAL ASSISTANT Josh Spiegel
PRODUCTION EDITOR Megan Emery
PHOTO EDITOR Sarah Bloom
SERIES & COVER DESIGNER Terry Mallon
LAYOUT Jennifer Krassy Peiler

A Haights Cross Communications 〜 Company

www.chelseahouse.com

First Printing

1 3 5 7 9 8 6 4 2

36242060339344
Library of Congress Cataloging-in-Publication Data

D'Orio, Wayne.
  Carol Moseley-Braun / by Wayne D'Orio.
    p. cm. -- (African-American leaders)
Summary: Profiles the first African-American woman to serve in the
United States Senate, Carol Moseley-Braun, who represented the state of
Illinois from 1992 through 1998. Includes bibliographical references and
index.
  ISBN 0-7910-7684-9
  1. Moseley-Braun, Carol, 1947---Juvenile literature. 2. African
American women legislators--Biography--Juvenile literature. 3.
Legislators--United States--Biography--Juvenile literature. 4. United
States. Congress. Senate--Biography--Juvenile literature. [1. Moseley-
Braun, Carol, 1947- 2. Legislators. 3. African Americans--Biography. 4.
Women--Biography.] I. Title. II. Series.
  E840.8.M67D67 2003
  328.73'092--dc22

                                                        2003012278

Table of Contents

INTRODUCTION

Beginning with the publication of the series *Black Americans of Achievement* nearly twenty years ago, Chelsea House Publishers made a commitment to publishing biographies for young adults that celebrated the lives of many of the country's most outstanding African Americans. The mix of individuals whose lives we covered was eclectic, to say the least. Some were well known—Dr. Martin Luther King, Jr., for example—although others we covered might be lesser known—Madam C.J. Walker, for example. Some—like the actor Danny Glover—were celebrities with legions of adoring fans. It mattered not what an individual's "star" quality might be, or how well known they were to the general public. What mattered was the life of the individual—their actions, their deeds, and, ultimately, their influence on the lives of others and our nation, as a whole. By telling the life stories of these unique Americans, we hoped to tell the story of how ordinary individuals are transformed by extraordinary circumstances to people of greatness. We hoped that the special lives we covered would inspire and encourage our young-adult readers to go out in the world and make a positive difference; and judging from the many wonderful letters that we have received over the years from students, librarians, and teachers about our *Black Americans of Achievement* biographies, we are certain that many of our readers did just that!

Now, some twenty years later, we are proud to release this new series of biographies, *African-American Leaders*, which we hope will make a similar mark on the lives of our young-adult readers. The individuals whose lives we cover in this first set of six books are all contemporary

African-American leaders. As these individuals are all living, the biographers made every attempt to interview their subjects so they could provide first-hand accounts and interesting anecdotes about each subject's life.

After reading about the likes of Henry Louis Gates, Jr., Cornel West, Condoleezza Rice, Carol Moseley-Braun, Eleanor Holmes Norton, and Benjamin Hooks, we think you will agree that the lives of these African-American leaders are remarkable. By overcoming the barriers that racism placed in their paths, they are an example of the power and resiliency of the human spirit and an inspiration to us all.

The Editor
Chelsea House Publishers

1

A Historic Victory

"People had seen the Senate in action and didn't like what they saw. The Senate had exposed itself and demystified itself. Most folks had thought of the U.S. Senate as this lofty body of great thinkers dealing with the issues of our time, and what they saw were some garden-variety politicians making bad speeches."

—Carol Moseley-Braun, "A Shock to the System,"
Los Angeles Times, March 1992

Sometimes the biggest event in your life happens when you're not even there. That's the way it was for Carol Moseley-Braun.

The turning point in Moseley-Braun's historic career occurred 700 miles away from her. On October 10, 1991, the 44-year-old Moseley-Braun was running the Cook County Recorder of Deeds office. This in itself was a big achievement.

Reason to smile: Carol Moseley-Braun addresses a crowd. In 1992, Moseley-Braun became the first African-American female member of the United States Senate.

She was the first woman and the first African-American to hold an executive office in Illinois's Cook County government.

But her life was about to change, and fast. On the next day, the United States Senate Judiciary Committee reopened hearings on Supreme Court nominee Clarence Thomas.

Three days and 35 hours of televised coverage later, the country, and especially Moseley-Braun, would be forever changed. Thirteen months later, Moseley-Braun, fueled by her and the nation's memory of those hearings, would become the first African-American woman to be elected to the U.S. Senate.

CLARENCE THOMAS V. ANITA HILL

The Thomas hearings were the talk of the summer of 1991 even before the entire country ended up debating whether Anita Hill was lying.

Thomas, at that time a federal appeals court judge, was President George H. Bush's nominee to the Supreme Court. Part of the controversy swirling around his nomination stemmed from the fact that Thomas, a staunch conservative, was slated to replace a liberal icon of the Court, Thurgood Marshall.

Civil rights and women's groups banded together to oppose Thomas, while the White House and Justice Department lawyers prepared to steel him for the inevitable barrage of questions.

The nomination process lasted for more than three months, including eight days of questioning by the 14-member Senate committee. During his questioning, Thomas was careful to avoid giving opponents any political opinions to oppose. He told the committee he had never discussed the controversial *Roe* v. *Wade* decision that made abortions legal. He gave little hint of how he might rule if appointed to the Supreme Court. But he survived. At the end of the questioning, the committee was deadlocked and passed his nomination onto the full Senate without a recommendation.

At the same time, Anita Hill, a former subordinate of Thomas's at the Department of Education and later the Equal Employment Opportunity Commission, said that Thomas had sexually harassed her. Hill's charge was made privately to the Judiciary Committee, but it was enough to have FBI agents continue to question her. When the details of her affidavit were leaked to the press and made public on October 6, 1991, the entire tenor of Thomas's confirmation changed. The Senate committee quickly reconvened its hearings on Thomas, and his bid to join the highest court in the country became a battle between him and Anita Hill.

Hill was a 35-year-old law professor at the University of Oklahoma who had worked with Thomas for three years at both the Department of Education and the Equal Employment Opportunity Commission. On live national television, in front of 30 million households, she repeated the charges she had made in private. She charged Thomas with discussing pornographic movies with her, asking her repeatedly for dates, and using coarse sexual language while talking with her.

Thomas refuted every charge Hill made. "I have not done or said the things Anita Hill has alleged," he said during the hearings. He called the proceedings a "high-tech lynching for uppity blacks." He told the commission, "I would have preferred an assassin's bullet to this kind of living hell." But he insisted he would "rather die than withdraw."

While Thomas was grilled, so was Hill. Before testimony began, Senator Alan Simpson warned Hill that she would face "real harassment, not the sexual kind," during her questioning. He later apologized for what he called his "arrogance" during the hearings. Hill testified for eight hours, answering questions, explaining her charges and discussing why she decided to make her complaint in the first place.

Republican Senator Arlen Specter of Pennsylvania said that Hill had committed "flat-out perjury." John Doggett III, a lawyer, testified that Hill might be suffering from an obscure mental illness called erotomania. This is defined as one person's excessive romantic interest in another person.

At the end, the Senate, filled with 98 men and two women, voted. Thomas was confirmed by a 52–48 margin.

The reaction was immediate. About 100 women demonstrated on the steps of the Capital, chanting, "We'll remember in November."

One of those watching the proceedings was Moseley-Braun. Shortly after the confirmation vote, she told the *Los Angeles Times*: "I was completely focused on how badly the process had failed. If the Senate had done its job right from the start, we all would have been spared the mess. And who were these guys anyway. Where were the women, the minorities, and the regular working people?"

Patricia Ireland, then executive vice president of the National Organization for Women, told *Maclean's* magazine: "Women across this country saw in a visceral way that we are not there and they don't respect us. Women have put on power suits, worn sensible shoes, and played the game by the rules, only to find themselves the victims of sexual harassment—and they're angry."

Moseley-Braun echoed those thoughts, adding "People had seen the Senate in action and didn't like what they saw. The Senate had exposed itself and demystified itself. Most folks had thought of the U.S. Senate as this lofty body of great thinkers dealing with the issues of our time, and what they saw were some garden-variety politicians making bad speeches."

She appeared on a public television talk show to share her feelings, and people started to encourage her to run for the Senate.

Illinois Senator Alan Dixon was one of 11 Democrats to vote for Thomas.

"The calls and the letters heated up, and the 'Draft Carol' press conferences started," she said.

Still, she was just one of three women whose names were put forward to face the incumbent Dixon.

When she made her official announcement to join the race on the local TV program, *Chicago Tonight*, she referred directly to the Thomas hearings.

"In examining the attitude and the judgment that this man [Thomas] has displayed [the Senate] not once raised an issue ... as fundamental to the whole question of women's equality as sexual harassment. Men just don't get it. It's an economic issue for women.... It has to do with equality in the workplace."

With little organization and less money, Moseley-Braun began to wage her campaign. She was one of three potential Senate candidates to make it to the party primary. Dixon and lawyer Alfred Hofeld were the favorites, and spent much of the campaign and debates slinging insults at each other. Moseley-Braun operated under the radar and built her grassroots support. She spent about $400,000, running only two television ads during the entire primary.

Despite being outspent by 10–1, Moseley-Braun went on to win the primary, receiving 38 percent of the vote. The incumbent Dixon took 35 percent, and Hofeld received 28 percent. Just like that, Moseley-Braun was the favorite in the heavily Democratic state.

Before the primary, the only person of note to back her campaign was women's activist Gloria Steinem. After the primary win, her friends increased. Massachusetts Senator Edward M. Kennedy, a Democrat, and Senate Majority Leader George Mitchell, a Democrat, met with her. Emily's List, a powerful organization that trumpets women politicians, gave her $200,000. Jan Wenner, the founder of *Rolling Stone* magazine, investment banker Felix Rohatyn, and novelist Gloria Naylor also contributed to her campaign contributions. Before she knew it, Moseley-Braun held a 3–1 fundraising lead over her Republican opponent Richard

Williamson.

In part because of the Senate hearings the previous summer, 1992 was shaping up as the Year of the Woman.

WINNING THE PRIZE

Moseley-Braun's political momentum continued when she electrified Democrats in 1992 with a six-minute speech at the party's national convention.

"We are proof that each person can make a difference, and together we will win.... With Bill Clinton and Al Gore, we can make 1992 the year we rediscover America."

Moseley-Braun joked that she would be a triple threat of diversity for the Senate, an African-American, a woman, and a member of the working class.

Her potential to make history if she won the race also helped. In the *Southtown Economist*, consultant David Axelrod said: "There's no question she gets a bounce from the convention. You won't see [Republican candidate] Rich Williamson on *Good Morning America*. He is something old and familiar. She represents the new and exciting. That's something he can't overcome."

But Moseley-Braun's political momentum would meet a bump in the road. Shortly before Election Day, Moseley-Braun was charged with mishandling $28,750 when family-owned land was sold in Alabama. The money had been deposited by Moseley-Braun, but should have been turned over to the state to help pay for her mother's nursing home bills. Moseley-Braun admitted her mistake and repaid the money.

Although the polls showed her with a lead near Election Day, some political watchers cautioned that an African-American candidate might garner residents' support in a poll, but not when the curtain of the voting booth was closed.

On Election Day, much like most of her campaign, she

During her campaign for the U.S. Senate, Moseley-Braun received support from several influential politicians. Here we see Moseley-Braun with Bill Clinton (left) and Al Gore (far left) at a 1992 campaign rally in Chicago.

again proved the experts wrong. She won a strong 10-point victory over Williamson, gaining support from a broad-based coalition. Men or women, minorities or white, voters backed Moseley-Braun and helped her make history.

Three other women won seats in the Senate during this election. In California, Barbara Boxer won a six-year term, and fellow Democrat Diane Feinstein won the final two years of a seat. The other woman to run successfully for the Senate in 1992 was Patty Murray of Washington.

On the day Moseley-Braun took office, she made a simple

2

Chicago Upbringing

> "Chicago was a very segregated city when I was born, but from the vantage point of 208 E. 41st Street, the world was multiracial, multicultural, and multiethnic. Women of color could be judge, like Edith Sampson, or elected officials, like Anna Langford, or the wives of presidents and kings, like Mrs. Houphouet-Boigny. Gender was no bar to achievement."
>
> —Carol Moseley-Braun, *Ebony*

Carol Moseley-Braun was born Carol Moseley on August 16, 1947, in Chicago, Illinois. Her mother, Edna Davie Moseley, born in 1922, attended St. Xavier College and Dillard University in New Orleans. Her father, Joseph John Moseley, was a Chicago policeman and later a corrections officer. Carol is one of four children born to Edna and Joseph. Her youngest brother Johnny died in 1986; her brother Joseph is a homicide detective in Chicago; and her sister Marsha is a cable television executive.

CITY	2000	1990
Gary-Hammond, Indiana	87	90
Chicago, Illinois	**83**	**86**
New York, New York	83	82
Philadelphia, Pennsylvania	75	78
St. Louis, Missouri	72	79

SOURCE: U.S. Census Bureau, analysis by Lewis Mumford Center, SUNY-Albany, Albany, N.Y.

Recent census data show that Chicago is still the heavily segregated city that it was when Moseley-Braun was growing up. These index numbers show the segregation of blacks v. whites in some of the nation's better-known cities. A higher index number denotes a higher degree of segregation.

In an article in *Ebony* magazine, Moseley-Braun remembered her parents as being "the perfect counterpoints to one another. He, the confrontational idealist, she, the accommodating realist."

Both parents did share the optimism of post-World War II America. Her father wanted to become a lawyer; her mother wanted to be a pioneer in the medical technology field. Both enjoyed music, the arts, and the "possibilities of freedom in this country," she said. But they had their differences.

Her father confronted the issue of race head-on, with intense pride for his heritage. He expected people to treat him fairly despite being a black man working in the 1950s.

As Moseley-Braun wrote in *Ebony*, "He liked to empha-size the professions, intellectual pursuits, the grand scale of world-class contributions.... He was certain of his obligation to raise children who would become part of the 'Talented Tenth' of Negro achievers." (In 1903, W.E.B. Du Bois said that the Negro race would be saved by the accomplishments of its exceptional members, the "Talented Tenth.")

Joseph Moseley was a well-rounded individual; he played seven instruments and spoke several languages. Moseley-Braun said his myriad interests "sparked my thirst for knowledge and for experiences. Just by way of example, we'd go to a different church every Sunday. We'd go to our own and then to another one.

"By the time I'd grown up, I'd already attended several synagogues, the Baha'I temple, all different kinds of Protestant denominations, as well as Catholic ones. That's the eclectic education he gave us," she told *NEA Today*.

BLACK RIGHTS IN THE 1800S

Joseph Moseley also believed strongly in the teachings of W.E.B. Du Bois. Du Bois was a black man born in 1868 who thought the race problem in the country was due to ignorance. Du Bois spent most of his life studying blacks, trying to accumulate as much knowledge as possible to "cure" prejudice.

Dr. Martin Luther King, Jr. wrote of Du Bois, "History cannot ignore W.E.B. Du Bois, because history has to reflect truth, and Dr. Du Bois was a tireless explorer and a gifted discoverer of social truths. His singular greatness lay in his quest for truth about his own people."

Part of his studies were to show the vast cultural development in Africa, a country some Americans had thought of as a cultural cipher. While employed as a sociology teacher at Atlanta University for 13 years, Du Bois also studied and wrote about a host of issues as they affected black people, including morality, urbanization, crime, business, church, and college. His book *Black Reconstruction* focused on the contributions blacks made during the redevelopment of the country after the Civil War. Another book, *Dusk at Dawn*, presented his views on Africans and the African-American's quest for freedom.

In 1906, he and 29 men formed what was called the Niagara Movement. This group set out to maintain and fight for the rights of Negro freedom and growth. Three years later, this group was merged with some white liberals into the National Association for the Advancement of Colored People.

Moseley-Braun's mother, who grew up in the South, was much more resigned to Jim Crow. Jim Crow described the far-reaching, institutional segregation that affected every aspect of American life. Schools, restaurants, public transportation, theaters, drinking fountains—virtually all public and many private facilities practiced total separation of the races. The state of Florida went so far as to require "Negro" and "white" textbooks, and in South Carolina black and white cottonmill workers were prohibited from looking out the same window.

Moseley-Braun's mother inspired her daughter by frequently telling her, "You can do anything." When Moseley-Braun wrote about her mother for *Ebony*, she said, "She wanted to make certain that we were not overly impressed with credentials and could actually 'do' something meaningful to earn a living."

Her mother believed in the philosophy of Booker T. Washington. Washington was a former slave who was the dominant figure in black public affairs from 1895 to his death in 1915. In 1881, he founded the Tuskegee Institute under a charter from the Alabama legislature. The all-black institute's primary goal was to train teachers, although it offered academic and vocational training in other areas. The students built their own buildings, produced their own food, and provided for most of their own basic necessities.

One of Washington's famous speeches, "The Atlanta Compromise Address," was delivered in 1895 before the Cotton States Exposition. Here Washington offered white Americans a compromise. He said blacks would agree to stay socially segregated if whites would help blacks progress financially and educationally.

Many blacks disagreed with this view, most famously W.E.B. Du Bois. Du Bois's 1903 book, *The Souls of Black Folks*, included a chapter titled "Of Booker T. Washington and Others." In it, he analyzed Washington's philosophy and explained why he disagreed with it.

Nevertheless, Washington remained conservative, counseling against civil rights and rejecting protests as a way to answer white lynchings and segregation.

Washington's autobiography, *Up From Slavery*, was published in 1901, and he became the chief black advisor to both presidents Theodore Roosevelt and William Howard Taft.

Moseley-Braun talked of her upbringing in an article she wrote for *Ebony* in November 1995. "They [her parents] raised us in a world that did not acknowledge or legitimize racism. Ethnic pride was part and parcel of that world. My maternal grandparents had been Garveyites and Muslims, 'race men' as they were called at the time—but it was an integrated, multiracial world nonetheless. Possibly, but not entirely because of music—our home saw a continual flow of people from diverse ethnic and racial communities. It was a meeting forum of equals, and sometimes they would joke about being a 'United Nations of 41st Street.' It was not until much later that I could figure out that this wasn't the least bit unusual."

Moseley-Braun continued, "Chicago was a very segregated city when I was born, but from the vantage point of 208 E. 41st Street, the world was multiracial, multicultural, and multiethnic. Women of color could be judges, like Edith Sampson, or elected officials, like Anna Langford, or the wives of presidents and kings, like Mrs. Houphouet-Boigny. Gender was no bar to achievement."

Sampson was the first African-American delegate to the United Nations. President Harry Truman appointed her in 1950. In 1962, Sampson was the first black woman elected judge in the United States when she won a seat as an associate judge on Chicago's domestic court.

Langford actively defended civil rights workers in the 1960s and joined Dr. Martin Luther King, Jr.'s Chicago civil rights marches. She became the first woman elected to the Chicago City Council when she won her 1971 election. Although she lost her reelection bid, she returned to the city council to win two more terms, in 1983 and 1991.

Mrs. Houphouet-Boigny's husband, Felix Houphouet-Boigny, was prime minister of Cote d'Ivoire in 1959. A year later, he was elected president and he went on to serve seven five-year terms.

Moseley-Braun and her three younger siblings attended public schools on the South Side of Chicago. All were strongly encouraged to go to college.

When Moseley-Braun was in her teens, her parents divorced and she went to live with her grandmother, who lived in a rough neighborhood in Chicago known as "Bucket of Blood."

"I had a chance to be part of the black experience on a lot of different levels," she said.

Her mother, Edna, suffered a stroke in 1976. She died in 1993 of lung cancer.

RACISM IN THE 1950s

When she was seven, on May 17, 1954, a major turning point in the nation's Civil Rights was won. The U.S. Supreme Court ruled on the case called *Brown v. Board of Education of Topeka*. This case was brought by a Topeka, Kansas minister, Rev. Oliver Brown, because he felt it was unfair that his daughter Linda had to walk across railroad tracks and wait for a rickety bus to take her to a school that was only for blacks. Several other lawsuits sought to declare the system of segregated schools illegal. This practice was known as separate but equal.

When the decision was handed down, Supreme Court Justice Earl Warren wrote: "Does segregation of children in public schools solely on the basis of race, even though the physical facilities and other tangible factors may be equal, deprive children of the minority group of equal educational opportunities?... We believe it does.... To separate them from others of similar age and qualifications solely because of their race generates a feeling of inferiority as to their status in the community that may affect their hearts and minds in a way very unlikely ever to be undone.

"We conclude, unanimously, that in the field of public education the doctrine of 'separate but equal' has no place. Separate educational facilities are inherently unequal."

This ruling led to violence, especially in Mississippi, thought to be the most supremacist and segregated state in the country. A new group called the Citizens' Council, or the "white-collar Klan" as the civil rights activists called them, formed to harass blacks.

Moseley-Braun learned a tough lesson when she was just eight. Emmett Till, a 14-year-old black boy from the South Side of Chicago, was sent to visit relatives near Money, Mississippi in the summer of 1955. Till spoke to a white

Murder suspects Roy Bryant (right) and J.W. Milam (second from right) descend the steps of the county courthouse in Greenwood, Mississippi in 1955. In spite of being identified as the men who murdered 14-year-old Emmett Till, the two suspects were acquitted by an all-white jury.

woman at a convenience store, supposedly saying "Bye, baby," as he left the store. Three days later, two white men picked up Till at his cousin Mose Wright's house. They lynched Till.

Although Till's body was mutilated, his mother insisted on an open-casket funeral. On the first day of his funeral, 2,000 people gathered to see his body and pay their respects.

The two men accused of killing Till, Roy Bryant and J.W. Milam, were charged with murder. In a historic trial, Mose Wright identified the two men as the people who took

Till from his house. It was one of the first times a black man had accused white men of such a serious crime in court.

Blacks and women were banned from serving on the jury. On September 23, 1955, the jury took little more than an hour to deliberate on the charges. Its verdict was simple: not guilty. One juror later told a newspaper reporter that the verdict wouldn't have taken so long if they hadn't stopped to drink soda pop.

While the news brought tears and grief to her house, it was then that Moseley-Braun first learned of how her mother's oldest sister had died. (Moseley-Braun's mother learned the meaning of prejudice early in life when her older sister was struck and killed by a truck in Alabama. The driver of the truck was white, and no charges were filed against him.)

"I learned that being a Negro made me more vulnerable," Moseley-Braun told *Ebony*. "I learned that my color was an identifying badge, which would shape the expectations of the world about me."

The backlash about the Till case resulted in a key moment in civil rights history. Less than four months after Till was murdered, Rosa Parks refused to give up her seat on a city bus in Montgomery, Alabama. When she was kicked off the bus, blacks responded by starting a bus boycott that lasted 381 days. This was the start of the Civil Rights movement.

Moseley-Braun showed her resolve early. She once staged a one-person sit-in at a restaurant that refused to serve her, and she had rocks thrown at her when she refused to leave a whites-only beach. She also marched in an all-white, Chicago neighborhood with Dr. Martin Luther King, Jr. in 1963 to protest segregation.

By the time she graduated from high school, Moseley-Braun had become galvanized by the Civil Rights movement.

She went on to study political science at the University of Illinois in Chicago, and then pursued a law degree at the University of Chicago Law School. It was there that she met her future husband, Michael Braun. The couple would have one child, Matthew, in 1977. They divorced in 1986.

3

A Political Start

"This country is on the brink of disaster. When you're going 90 miles per hour over a cliff you don't stay the course, you change directions."

—Carol Moseley-Braun, *Newsmakers*

Moseley-Braun's career in politics began when she volunteered to help Harold Washington's campaign for Illinois state legislature. Washington won the election.

In 1978, Moseley-Braun took the leap from the sidelines to the arena when her Hyde Park neighbor, Kay Clement, urged the then 31-year-old mother to run as a state representative.

She ran for the seat that Robert Mann was leaving. Mann, a noted liberal, realized that Moseley-Braun certainly had the style and viewpoint to succeed him. He told the *Los Angeles Times* that when he first met Moseley-Braun, "She was well-spoken, congenial, and

This picture of Senator Moseley-Braun was taken at a 1992 meeting of Democratic Party senators. As a lawmaker, Moseley-Braun became known for her debating skills and her passionate support for education.

I thought she had the character to continue on in the tradition of us [rebels]."

Moseley-Braun defeated 11 other candidates for the seat.

Moseley-Braun quickly became known for two things as a young legislator: her ability to debate effectively, and her passion for education.

She was the chief sponsor of the state's 1985 Urban Schools Improvement Act, a law that helped create parents' councils at every city school. In addition, Braun sponsored every school funding bill for eight consecutive years, from 1980 to 1987.

The Schools Improvement Act even gave parents and community councils the power to veto budgets and the ability to hire and fire teachers and principals. In a 1993 interview with *NEA Today* (the official magazine of the National Education Association), Moseley-Braun said the legislation might have gone too far.

"I think [the bill] came about because the education establishment was so resistant to change and so resistant to bringing parents into the mix and letting them have some role to play.

"Overall, I'm pleased the decision-making process is opening up, allowing more voices—parents and teachers— to be heard." Moseley-Braun served 11 years in the state legislature, eventually being named the assistant majority leader. This meant she was the floor leader for Harold Washington, who had become the city's mayor.

Washington served 12 years in the state House of Representatives, four years in the state Senate, and two terms and four years in the U.S. House of Representatives.

He won a close race to become Chicago's first black mayor, first edging incumbent Mayor Jane Byrne, and then defeating Bernard Epton in the general election. Four years later, although he had overseen an unpopular $70 million property tax increase, he was reelected easily. Less than a month after his 1987 win for a second term as mayor, he had a heart attack and died.

Moseley-Braun was not afraid to go against people in her party or people she had worked for if she believed her cause was right. While in the state legislature, she success- fully sued five Democratic leaders over discriminatory redistricting policies.

She broke away from Washington's influence when she unsuccessfully ran for lieutenant governor without his endorsement.

"Her years and experience in the legislature were key," said Ingrid Cravens, a community activist and then president of the Decatur NAACP. "To get things done, Carol learned to work with the other legislators. She's been a maverick on certain issues, but she also understands how the system works, and that you have to depend on a broad support base to get things done. She's learned the give-and-take from a legislative standpoint. She has truly gone to school in this arena," Cravens told *Essence*.

Moseley-Braun's time in the state legislature marked her as an outspoken Equal Rights Amendment supporter, an ardent feminist, and even though she was raised a Catholic, firmly pro-choice (i.e., a believer that women should be free to choose when or if they will bear a child).

TAKING ON A NEW CHALLENGE

In 1988, she sought a change. Looking for a job closer to home to help her care for her son and her sick mother, Moseley-Braun completed her first political breakthrough when she ran for, and won handily, the position of Cook County Recorder of Deeds. She replaced fellow Democrat Harry Yourell in the $50,000-a-year post.

Moseley-Braun was the first woman, and the first African American, to hold elected office in the county.

The Recorder of Deeds office was a sleepy post with an antiquated system of record keeping when she took over. The office, which employed 300 people and had an annual budget of $8 million, was losing money before she arrived.

In short order, she brought mass computerization to the office, revolutionizing the way it ran. The Recorder of Deeds office was soon showing a profit.

One person from the local realtor's association told the *Los Angeles Times* that the office was "not a dungeon anymore. You don't have to carry your own candle."

In 1991, just as Moseley-Braun was deciding whether she should run for a second term in her office, President George H.W. Bush nominated Judge Clarence Thomas for the U.S. Supreme Court.

The uproar over Thomas's nomination lasted for three months even before his hearing started in the U.S. Senate.

Although he declined to discuss his views on many issues when questioned, Democrats assailed Thomas as being too conservative.

But when Anita Hill entered the confirmation hearings, everything changed. Hill charged Thomas with sexual harassment, and during three days of testimony in front of the Senate's Judiciary Committee, both Hill and Thomas were subjected to intense questioning.

With what felt like the entire nation watching, the Senate confirmed Thomas by a 52–48 vote. Eleven Democrats, including Illinois Senator Alan Dixon, voted for Thomas.

ENTERING THE PRIMARY

Moseley-Braun was one of thousands of Americans outraged by the confirmation. She talked to the *Los Angeles Times* about her feelings, and appeared on a local television show.

In part, she said: "People had seen the Senate in action and didn't like what they saw. The Senate had exposed itself and demystified itself. Most folks had thought of the

U.S. Senate as this lofty body of great thinkers dealing with the issues of our time, and what they saw were some garden-variety politicians making bad speeches."

People started urging her to run for Dixon's Senate seat, which was up in 1992.

Although the National Organization for Women had immediately made the claim that these proceedings would result in more women being elected, Moseley-Braun faced an uphill battle.

Dixon was undefeated in his 43-year political career. Known as "The Pal," he was the champion vote getter in all of Illinois.

For a campaign that would end with one of the highest profiles during the 1992 elections, Moseley-Braun's run at history began quietly.

Despite 11 years in state government, only two members of the Illinois congressional delegation endorsed her. Illinois' other senator, Paul Simon, supported Dixon although Moseley-Braun had co-chaired his 1990 campaign.

During the primary, Simon told the *New Republic*, "If Carol would ask me my advice, my advice would be 'Don't run.' At some point, if Alan or I retire, then that's a point where perhaps we can provide a little more diversity in the Senate."

When she won the primary, Simon reconsidered his comments and even appeared in one of Moseley-Braun's campaign videos. "There are 14 of us on that Senate Judiciary Committee. We are all white. We are all male. I think if we had had Carol Moseley-Braun on that commit-tee, we would not have confirmed Clarence Thomas."

Moseley-Braun's campaign got some attention for its grassroots nature, with the candidate traveling throughout the state to meet with many different types of organizations.

But she got as much notice in the press for her campaign's disorganization, its lack of money, and charges of mismanagement. Halfway through the primary, her campaign manager left because she needed heart surgery, her deputy campaign manager left to run for a judgeship, and her press secretary's multiple sclerosis flared up.

"I was ready to throw in the towel, go practice law and forget this," Braun said looking back after her historic win.

Two weeks before the primary, an editorial in the *Chicago Tribune* endorsed Dixon and said of her campaign: "It has been disappointing to watch Carol Braun's campaign unfold and then unravel. She has struggled to remain politically competitive and seems to be losing the fight."

One day she was scheduled for three events at the same time. Later that day, she met Kgosie Matthews. Matthews was a South African who had been raised and educated in England. He had attended the Kennedy School of Government at Harvard and had been a special assistant to Rev. Jesse Jackson for four years. By the end of their lunch meeting, Matthews had agreed to run her campaign.

Matthews was taken with Moseley-Braun's ability to reach different constituencies.

"Carol's constituency transcends racial and sexual boundaries. She has certainly the best crossover appeal of any candidate I've seen in American politics. She just defies description. I don't think there's any constituency that's a hard nut [for her] to crack."

A good example of Moseley-Braun's political deftness can be seen in her handling of leaders in the Jewish community. Moseley-Braun was unafraid of telling leaders in the Jewish community that while she was a strong supporter of Israel, she did not support the sale of Israeli arms to South Africa. She was clear to tell the group that she wasn't waffling on her position; she was just setting a limit to what she believed was right.

This same tack of laying her cards on the table has also been used by Moseley-Braun when asked about the civil rights activist Rev. Jesse Jackson and Nation of Islam leader Minister Louis Farrakhan. (Both Jackson and Farrakhan have been known to have made anti-semitic remarks.) "Why am I being asked about Jesse Jackson? Because he lives in my neighborhood? Because we're both black? A black is held to a different, higher standard, and it pisses me off. Are we going to allow racists to paint every black candidate as anti-Semitic, or are we going to say, 'Wait a minute.' I will not denounce anybody. I do not believe in personal denunciations. They smack of McCarthyism to me."

One of the breaks Moseley-Braun received in her bid for Dixon's Senate seat was the presence of a third candidate in the race, Alfred Hofeld. Hofeld was a multimillionaire personal injury and products liability lawyer, but a political neophyte. While Dixon had a well-funded campaign chest, Hofeld spent more than $5 million of his own money on advertisements that portrayed Dixon in a negative light.

Hofeld claimed Dixon was out of touch with his constituents and too concerned with special-interest groups. Dixon fired back with $2 million worth of his own commercials, defending himself and criticizing Hofeld.

On the sidelines sat Moseley-Braun. She spent about $400,000 on her entire campaign, and could only afford two television commercials, both of which ran the week before the primary. She summed up whatever momentum she had by saying, "This country is on the brink of disaster. When you're going 90 miles per hour over a cliff you don't stay the course, you change directions."

A turning point in her early campaign was a television debate during which Dixon and Hofeld criticized each other excessively, leaving Moseley-Braun as a sort of sensible alternative.

This performance caught the eye of women's activist Gloria Steinem. Steinem's reputation and support helped Moseley-Braun capture the attention of the white liberal voters in Illinois.

Although Dixon was a Democrat, he had sided with President George H.W. Bush 58 percent of the time in 1991—more than any other northern Democrat in the Senate. Dixon had a hard time explaining why he favored so many policies that ended up hurting people in Illinois. While the entire country was in the midst of a recession in 1992, Illinois was hit harder than most other states.

In 1991, the country was in the middle of a recession, and Moseley-Braun made the cornerstones of her campaign job creation, universal health care, and increased federal funding for education.

Moseley-Braun also continued to look back at the 1991 Thomas hearings, telling the *Nation*, "What inspires me is that that anger is focused much more against a system of ideological patronage and a Billionaire Boys Club whose abandonment of domestic policy has brought us to a social and economic precipice."

When the primary finally arrived, so did Moseley-Braun. Although she got less than 40 percent of the vote, she edged out both the incumbent Dixon and newcomer

Hofeld. Moseley-Braun gathered 38 percent of the vote, Dixon took 35 percent, and Hofeld captured 28 percent.

She dismissed talk that the three-way race was the only way she could have captured the Democratic nomination. "People are ready for a change. That's why I won," she said.

In the heavily Democratic state of Illinois, Moseley-Braun went from underdog to overwhelming favorite.

4

DIVERSIFYING THE SENATE

"We are proof that each person can make a difference, and together we will win. ... With Bill Clinton and Al Gore, we can make 1992 the year we rediscover America."

—Carol Moseley-Braun, *Minneapolis Star Tribune*

Given America's history with slavery and racial segregation, it may seem surprising that, well before Moseley-Braun's election to the U.S. Senate, other African Americans had made their mark on this prestigious and powerful governing body many years before.

Certainly, the inclusion of African Americans in the U.S. Senate marked a milestone in the long struggle for racial equality in America; for the Senate is, perhaps, the most powerful governing body in the nation. To understand the great power held by the Senate, consider that, unlike the U.S. House of Representatives, the Senate comprises

HEROES OF THE COLORED RACE.

A portrait of Hiram R. Revels (right) with two other outstanding African-American leaders, Frederick Douglass (center) and Blanche K. Bruce (left). In 1870, Revels became the first African American to serve in the U.S. Senate.

two members from each State in the country. (A state's Representatives, on the other hand, are accorded on the basis of the state's poulation in relation to the entire country. This means that a highly populated state like California might have 52 House seats, while Rhode Island might only have 2.) Although both the House and Senate must pass a bill for it to become law, it is the Senate that votes on court appointments, cabinet members, ambassadors, and other high-ranking positions. In addition, the Senate approves treaties with foreign countries, and judges cases of impeachment.

The first black member of the Senate was Hiram R. Revels from Mississippi, who served from 1870 to 1871. Revels was born in 1822 in Fayetteville, North Carolina. When the Civil War started in 1861, Revels supported the Union cause in Maryland, a border state with divided loyalties between the Union and the Confederate armies. At the age of 39, Revels aided in the organization of two regiments of African-American troops, and fought in the Campaign of Vicksburg in Mississippi.

When he was elected to the state senate in 1869, Revels sought to restore voting rights and the right to hold office for former confederates. He also advocated desegregation in schools and on the railroad. When he left the Senate, just 13 months later, he was named the president of Alcorn College in Mississippi. It was the state's first college for blacks.

Just four years after Revels completed his Senate stint, Blanche K. Bruce of Mississippi was elected to serve in the U.S. Senate. His six-year term, from 1875 to 1881, marked the first time a black man had served a full term in the Senate.

Bruce, born into slavery near Farmville, Virginia, in 1841, organized Missouri's first school for blacks in 1864. Five years later, he moved to Mississippi and became a wealthy landowner who was involved in local politics.

When the Mississippi legislature voted him into the Senate, he was rebuffed by his fellow Mississippi colleague, James L. Alcorn.

During his time in the Senate, Bruce encouraged the government to be more generous in giving land grants to black emigrants. He also tried to desegregate the country's army, and asked for a Senate inquiry into the violent Mississippi elections of 1875. At the 1880 Republican convention in Chicago, Bruce served briefly as presiding officer and received eight votes for vice president.

In 2002, the Senate commissioned a new portrait of Bruce to be displayed in the nation's Capitol. At the unveiling on September 17, Senator Christopher Dodd, a Democrat from Connecticut, said: "Blance Bruce's place in this building—the closest thing America has to a national shrine to democracy—reflects one person's struggle for freedom; the freedom that this glorious domed building represents to the world."

Following Bruce's illustrious six-year Senate term, however, the Senate would remain all-white for 85 years. Finally, in 1966, the third black man to serve in the U.S. Senate, Edward W. Brooke of Massachusetts, was elected. Brooke served in the Senate from 1966 to 1978.

Brooke, who was born in 1919 in Washington, D.C., became the first African American to be popularly elected to the Senate. A successful Boston lawyer, Bruce failed twice in 1950 and 1952 to win a seat in the state legislature. In 1960, he ran for, but lost, the Massachusetts Secretary of State office.

Two years later, however, he was elected attorney general of Massachusetts, and he won reelection in 1964. Bruce was known as a vigorous prosecutor of organized crime.

In 1966, three years after Dr. Martin Luther King, Jr.'s famous "I have a dream" speech in Washington, D.C., Brooke won his election to the Senate by 500,000 votes.

He was a soft-spoken moderate on civil rights, but a leader of the Republican's progressive wing.

Six years later, in 1972, Brooke was reelected by a wide margin. During his time in Washington, he fought to create low-income housing and to boost the nation's minimum wage. He also promoted the creation of more mass transit systems and the idea of racial equality in the South.

In 1978, however, he lost his reelection bid, in part because of personal problems including a divorce, and accusations of financial improprieties.

BECOMING A DEMOCRATIC FAVORITE

When the surprise of the primary set in, the only thing standing between Moseley-Braun and history was the Republican Richard Williamson. Williamson was a one-time assistant secretary of state in the Reagan administration.

The primary win did more than change Moseley-Braun from underdog to favorite—it brought her national attention from TV shows and newspapers. That, in turn, led to the type of support from prominent Democrats that she could only have dreamed of before the primary.

When running against Dixon, Moseley-Braun couldn't get Illinois Senator Paul Simon to back her. Now that she was the party's choice in the upcoming election, she quickly met with Massachusetts Senator Edward M. Kennedy and Senate Majority Leader George J. Mitchell.

Fundraising became considerably easier. Emily's List, an organization that supports female political candidates, gave her $200,000. Jan Wenner, founder of *Rolling Stone* magazine; investment banker Felix Rohatyn; and Hyatt Hotels heiresses Marian and Penny Pritzker also contributed money to her campaign.

While her primary win was waged with about $40,000, Moseley-Braun had a war chest of more than $6 million to take on Williamson. Moseley-Braun went from being the underfunded, poorly managed candidate, to the favorite who suddenly had a lot more money than her opponent.

Although her race was restricted to Illinois, the potential history of her election made Moseley-Braun a national figure.

"Women around the country feel emotionally and politically invested in this campaign," said Ann Lewis, the former policy director for the Democratic National Party. Speaking to the *Southtown Economist*, she said that to other women, Moseley-Braun's success "was like waking up in the morning and finding a muscle that you didn't know you had. [The victory] set off a wave of energy and a climate that's still going."

Moseley-Braun parlayed this strength into getting a speech at the Democratic National Convention that summer. Her six-minute talk covered her working-class roots. In part, she said: "Our cities can be rebuilt, our roads reconstructed, our environment saved, and health care provided for every American when we remember that the people who serve in high public office are the servants and not the masters of the people who elect them."

Consultant David Axelrod said there was no doubt Moseley-Braun's presence and her exciting campaign were boosts that her opponent couldn't match. In the *Southtown Economist*, he said: "There's no question she gets a bounce from the convention. You won't see Republican candidate Rich Williamson on *Good Morning America*. He is something old and familiar. She represents the new and exciting. That's something he can't overcome."

As much momentum as Moseley-Braun had on her side, there was more. 1992 was shaping up as The Year of the Woman. A record number of women were competing for national seats. In the Senate alone, four women were trying to win seats. During Thomas's confirmation hearing the entire 100-member Senate had just two women.

Moseley-Braun alluded to the other Democratic women candidates when she told the *Minneapolis Star Tribune*, "We are proof that each person can make a difference, and together we will win.... With Bill Clinton and Al Gore, we can make 1992 the year we rediscover America."

When asked about the historic possibilities of her Senate bid, Moseley-Braun said: "It would be wonderful if the great state of Illinois sent the first African-American woman to the U.S. Senate. But the fact is, I'm also the most qualified candidate for the job."

In an interview with the *Boston Globe*, Moseley-Braun said: "It's a historic candidacy and we're going to make history. The state is ready and willing to strike a blow for revitalizing our democracy and opening the doors to the Senate."

THE BATTLE TO THE END

Williamson was a political neophyte, initially recruited by the Republican party with the idea of being a longshot against the incumbent Alan Dixon.

Just two months before the election, in September, 1992, Moseley-Braun had opened up a 34-point lead on Williamson. Then the campaign got interesting.

For most of the campaign, Williamson was trying to paint Moseley-Braun as a big-spending, big-taxing liberal. For her part, she was to the left of the Democratic party. She favored a tax hike for the top one percent of wage earners, wanted $100 billion slashed from defense spending, and was pushing to institute a universal health-care plan.

The complexion of the race changed when a local television reporter from station WMAQ-TV in Chicago got a copy of a cancelled check from Moseley-Braun. Three years earlier, owners of property in Alabama had decided to sell timber harvesting rights to the property. Moseley-Braun's mother Edna, who was in a nursing home at the time, was one of the property's owners.

Because Edna Moseley was supported by Medicaid, the money from the sale should have been reported to Medicaid as her income. This would have reduced the amount of Medicaid money she received.

Instead the money was split between Moseley-Braun, her sister and her brother. Moseley-Braun's cut of the sale was $28,750.

Williamson jumped on the news. He had already charged Moseley-Braun with a variety of ethical lapses, but this story was bigger. He campaigned against her by saying the Medicaid scandal was part of a "pattern of deception" that raised the "question of trust" with Moseley-Braun.

His supporters flat-out charged her with "Medicaid fraud."

Williamson's campaign had already compared Moseley-Braun to Gus Savage, a notoriously anti-Semitic black congressman, and to Jesse Jackson, who uttered his infamous "Hymietown" remark eight years earlier.

Williamson started gaining momentum, taking at least 10 points off Moseley-Braun's lead in less than a month.

To counteract his momentum, Moseley-Braun issued a statement in which she answered the charges of financial irregularities.

"I fully believe that everything we did was in accordance with the law and the regulations. At no time was there any attempt to deprive the Department of Public Aid, the state, the nursing home or any other person of any money rightfully due them."

She continued her statement. "In hindsight, perhaps I should have taken greater control of the reporting requirements....I should have second-guessed my mother."

While Williamson campaigned hard against her, Moseley-Braun did not shy away from his attacks.

At one point, she described Williamson's strategy as trying to "frighten people with the image of a bomb-throwing welfare mother running for Senate."

During a debate, Moseley-Braun regained the momentum of her campaign when she outperformed Williamson face-to-face. Referencing his frequent attack ads, she dubbed him the "Freddy Krueger of Illinois politics."

In the days leading up to the campaign, Moseley-Braun's lead hovered at about 20 percent, with 50 percent of the voters saying they favored her and 30 percent preferring Williamson.

But pundits argued that this lead may not have been as safe as it looked. When an African-American candidate is involved, some people are uncomfortable telling pollsters their opinions because they are afraid to appear to be racist if they don't support the minority candidate.

When the election came, the state's message was clear. Moseley-Braun won by a convincing 10 percent of the vote, garnering support from women and minorities, but also from other groups throughout the state of Illinois.

On the day she took office, Moseley-Braun made a simple statement. "By my presence, the U.S. Senate will change," she vowed.

It didn't take long for these words to be proven right.

5

Instant Success

"I have to tell you, this vote [renewing the patent to the symbol of the United Daughters of the Confederacy] is about race. It is about racial symbolism. It is about racial symbols, the racial past, and the single most painful episode in American history."
—Carol Moseley-Braun, *Argumentation and Advocacy*

As if her historic campaign win wasn't enough to satisfy her, Moseley-Braun quickly got another piece of good news.

Shortly after being sworn in, she was appointed to the Senate's Judiciary Committee. This was the same committee that had held the Clarence Thomas hearings in 1991—the very group whose exclusiveness sparked Moseley-Braun's decision to run in the first place.

Life wasn't perfect however, as Moseley-Braun settled into her new life. During her campaign, two women on her

Senator under fire: At a 1993 press conference, Senator Moseley-Braun faced tough questions about her mishandling of $28,750 that should have been turned over to the state to help pay for her mother's nursing home bills. The senator admitted her mistake and repaid the money.

staff accused campaign manager Kgosie Matthews of sexual harassment. At the time, Matthews and Moseley-Braun were romantically linked. Less than three months later, she would become engaged to him, but the two would never get married.

Moseley-Braun said she hired a lawyer to look into the charges, but found them groundless.

Reporters also questioned Moseley-Braun about her new apartment, her new Jeep, and the three-week-long vacation she took to Africa and England after the election.

After her first week on Capitol Hill, a weary Moseley-Braun said, "If this is a honeymoon, I'm going to divorce."

But these issues quickly faded into the background compared to what happened on July 22, 1993. It was on this day that Moseley-Braun made a stand that stamped what type of senator she would be, a stand that at once sent out warnings to people who would try to fight her, and made those on her side feel like she would protect them with all her abilities.

While events like these are rare enough in the Senate, they are unheard of coming from a freshman senator who is just six months into her term. It's likely that some of the other senators on the floor that day thought Moseley-Braun should still be learning her way around the halls of the Capitol rather than taking on one of the body's oldest members.

TAKING ON JESSE HELMS

While at a separate confirmation hearing, Moseley-Braun was called out of the room and told that Senator Jesse Helms, a Republican from North Carolina, had added an amendment to a bill on National Service.

Helms' attachment would have extended a patent to the symbol of the United Daughters of the Confederacy. Although the Senate's Judiciary Committee had already voted to refuse the patent renewal, Helms said the action "was an unintended rebuke unfairly aimed at about 24,000 ladies who belong to the United Daughters of the Confederacy, most of them elderly, all of them gentle souls who meet together and work together as unpaid volunteers at veterans hospitals and many, many other places."

What Helms didn't say, but what other members of the Senate knew, was that the design the Daughters were looking to get renewed contained the Confederate flag. Since this flag was used on the losing side of the Civil War, and the key issue in that war was the legality of using slaves, many people today associate the Confederate flag as part of a movement to segregate blacks and other minorities while declaring that the white race is superior.

The Confederate constitution said in part: "It's cornerstone rests upon the great truth that the Negro is not equal to the white man, that slavery, subordination to the superior race, is his natural and moral condition."

Moseley-Braun's first speech on this issue pointed out that the patent extension wasn't needed, that adding it to the bill under consideration wasn't relevant, and that the Daughters group had other options to protect its design. She also said, "The fact of the matter is the emblems of the Confederacy have meaning to Americans even 100 years after the end of the Civil War."

•   •   •

Helms referred to her speech as "tactics" and urged his fellow senators to grant an extension.

Although Helms had been in the Senate for 20 years, and Moseley-Braun for just six months, other senators agreed with the junior senator from Illinois and spoke in favor of allowing her to speak for the African-American race.

Senator Patty Murray of Washington said, "I know her sense of frustration. I recognize her outrage. As a woman, I share some understanding of her situation. But I cannot know her sense of isolation being the only African American in this body."

Senator Joseph Biden of Delaware called Moseley-Braun "the one single voice speaking for millions and millions of voices in this country who feel disenfranchised."

Senator Jesse Helms speaks during a campaign for reelection. During Senator Moseley-Braun's first year in office, she stood up to the powerful Senator Helms by criticizing his support for the Confederate flag.

The vote to table the measure was defeated by four votes, 52–48. Moseley-Braun was stunned, but she quickly recovered and claimed the floor. What followed is perhaps the moment for which Moseley-Braun's political career is best remembered. A moment that brought together her strong speaking skills, her sense of outrage as an African American who felt like her race wasn't being represented, and her ability to sway her peers with her arguments.

She began her second speech on the subject mentioning the dry topics she covered the first time. "What I did not talk about and what I am constrained now to talk about with no small degree of emotion is the symbolism of what this vote really means.

"I have to tell you, this vote is about race. It is about racial symbolism. It is about racial symbols, the racial past, and the single most painful episode in American history."

She continued. "I have to, on many occasions, as the only African American here, constrain myself to be calm, to be laid back, to talk about these issues in very intellectual, non-emotional terms, and that is what I do on a regular basis.

"The issue is not whether or not Americans, such as myself, who believe in the promise of this country, who feel strongly and who are patriots in this country, will have to suffer the indignity of being reminded time and time again, that at one point in this country's history, we were human chattel. We were property. We could be traded, bought, and sold."

In tears, she continued. "There are those who would keep us slipping back into the darkness of division, into the snake pit of racial hatred, of racial antagonism and of support for symbols—symbols of the struggle to keep African Americans, Americans of African descent, in bondage."

She continued with her speech. "On this issue, there can be no consensus. It is an outrage. It is an insult. It is absolutely unacceptable to me and to millions of Americans, black and white, that we would put the imprimatur of the United States Senate on a symbol of this kind of idea."

Moseley-Braun had shifted the debate from a dry recounting of facts and legal precedent, into senators' personal feelings toward slavery and the country's history in racism. The *Washington Post* wrote: "Her words...

eloquent and angry...bristling with outrage...prompted an outpouring of emotion and personal expressions about racism that are rarely heard in the Senate."

Senator Bill Bradley, a Democrat from New Jersey, joined Moseley-Braun's argument. He lectured the Republican senators saying, "I appeal to my colleagues on the other side of the aisle who, in a legalistic argument, would make the case but put in a human context, in 1993, in the United States, it has a perverse impact."

Senator John Danforth summed up how the issue had gone from a rather routine one to a stand on one of the biggest issues still facing the country. "It became clear after the first vote that this was a highly symbolic question and that the symbolism that we were supposed to vote on was how we felt about racism in America," he said.

Perhaps the most stirring speech of the day, outside of Moseley-Braun's, was from Howell Herin of Alabama. He told of his family's history with the Confederacy. Then he said: "But I revere my family, and I respect those who thought whatever they were doing was right at that particular time in our nation's history. But we live today in a different world. We live in a nation that every day is trying to heal the scars of racism that have occurred in the past."

One of the Senate's longest standing members, Democrat Daniel Patrick Moynihan from New York, said, "...in my 17 years in this body, I have been not so moved as by her statement. She spoke of what in Christian faith would be called an epiphany, a sudden shining through of an internal reality that had not been there. I don't think the Senate knew it could do what it has just done."

Another minority in the Senate, Ben Nighthorse Campbell, a Native American from Colorado, said: "I just want Carol Moseley-Braun to know that she is not alone in this fight. The history of this country has not been good to African Americans and perhaps not good to American Indians either. So I understand that sensitivity."

The debate veered back toward the upcoming vote when Moseley-Braun got the floor again and pleaded with Senate members to rethink their stance on this issue. "I would encourage my colleagues on both sides of the aisle, Republican and Democrat, those who thought, 'Well, we are just going to do this, you know, because it is no big deal,' to understand what a very big deal indeed it is."

Senator Howard Heflin of Alabama voted against tabling the issue. But after this raft of speeches in the Senate, he spoke for those opposed, and for those who fought to make the Confederacy work more than 130 years ago. "I feel strongly that if they were alive today, they would stand for what is right and honorable, and they would agree with me that it is time to move forward in our nation's history."

Senator John Chafee of Rhode Island admitted running to the chamber from lunch as word of the debate began to spread. "I must say, regrettably, rarely on this floor are minds changed. All too often nobody is here listening, or, if people are listening, they are only listening so they can jump up and give their speech without paying a great deal of heed to the speeches that have gone previously."

The debate wrapped up as Republican Senator Robert Bennett of Utah said, "A large number of Republicans did not realize the greater implications of what had just happened [when they voted not to table the Daughters' request]. I was one of those who, as I circulated among my fellow Republicans, said, 'Do you understand what we have just done?' They said no, and I said I intend to make a motion to reconsider."

SPEAKING ABOUT RACE, CHANGING MINDS

The vote to reconsider tabling the amendment passed by a 75–25 vote, meaning that Moseley-Braun and the other senators' passionate speeches would result in 27 people changing their vote.

Even the senators who voted against Moseley-Braun felt compelled to explain their actions. Senator Connie Mack of Florida said, "I want to be absolutely clear about the intentions behind the two votes I cast today…because I reject the notion that the issue before the Senate was one of racism."

Robert Byrd of West Virgina said he understood Moseley-Braun and others' feelings about the symbolism in the Daughters' symbol, but that he felt the Confederacy "is part of American history."

Senator Moynihan summed up the day's extraordinary debate when he said, "I do not think the Senate knew it could do what it has just done."

The *New York Times* hailed Moseley-Braun's message, saying she "woke up a sleeping Senate to the unthinking way the white majority can offend minority Americans."

USA Today went even further, saying that Moseley-Braun "signaled a new day in the Senate, serving notice that she will not let what she sees as racism go unchallenged." The paper went on to say that the freshman senator's stand "made her a celebrity in a chamber that prides itself on courage, oratory, and leadership."

Although the final vote put this issue to rest once and for all in the Senate, the impact of the day's events were not soon forgotten by any of the senators who participated in that debate. While Jesse Helms was silent during most of the rhetoric about his proposal, he tried to get the last word in two weeks after the vote.

Helms found himself on an elevator with Moseley-Braun and he used the occasion to start singing "Dixie."

"He started to sing, 'I wish I was in the land of cotton …'" Moseley-Braun told an audience from the National Urban League. Helms then glanced at the freshman senator from Illinois and reportedly said, "I'm going to make her cry. I'm going to sing 'Dixie' until she cries."

Moseley-Braun shot back, "Senator Helms, your singing would make me cry if you sang 'Rock of Ages.'"

Many Americans find "Dixie" suggestive of pre-Civil War slavery, but also of the segregation that was widespread in the 1950s and 1960s. During the days of civil rights fights, Dixie was a rallying song for those fighting integration. Helms was a vocal opponent of racial equality at that time.

Representative James E. Clyburn, a Democrat from South Carolina, is a black man who fought the civil rights battles in the 1960s. He said: "Any gentlemanly white person would never do that. Most gentlemanly white people would not intentionally antagonize or harass a woman, be she black or white, and what he was doing was harassing that woman," Clyburn said.

Senator Alan Simpson, a Republican from Wyoming, said the two senators were probably joking. "She's got a pretty powerful strong sense of humor in her own way, and so does Jesse," said Simpson, a friend of Helms. "I've never seen him—especially in the presence of women—do anything that was other than civil and courteous. I doubt there was any rancorous nature to it."

6

The 1992 Breakthrough

> "Education, education, education. Education really will
> become the difference between the 'haves' and the
> 'have-nots' in the twenty-first century. Elementary and
> secondary education give children the opportunity
> to get literate, come out able to read, write and 'cipher,'
> as my grandmother used to say."
> —Carol Moseley-Braun, Chideya, *Essence*, October 1998

The 1992 elections were notable for much more than Moseley-Braun's election. In what the media dubbed the Year of the Woman, the Senate did see a vast increase in its female membership.

Before the 1992 elections, the 100-person body had just two women, Republican Nancy Kassebaum of Kansas and Barbara Ann Mikulski, a Democrat from Maryland.

Kassebaum won election to the Senate in 1978 and won two more terms. In all, she served from 1978 to 1997.

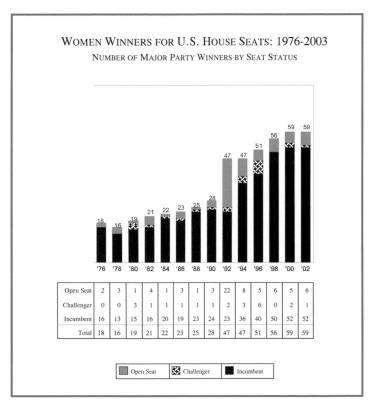

WOMEN WINNERS FOR U.S. HOUSE SEATS: 1976-2003

NUMBER OF MAJOR PARTY WINNERS BY SEAT STATUS

	'76	'78	'80	'82	'84	'86	'88	'90	'92	'94	'96	'98	'00	'02
Open Seat	2	3	1	4	1	3	1	3	22	8	5	6	5	6
Challenger	0	0	3	1	1	1	1	1	2	3	6	0	2	1
Incumbent	16	13	15	16	20	19	23	24	23	36	40	50	52	52
Total	18	16	19	21	22	23	25	28	47	47	51	56	59	59

Open Seat   Challenger   Incumbent

The Year of the Woman: The 1992 elections saw a significant increase in the number of female office holder in the U.S. House of Representatives.

Mikulski first served in the U.S. House of Representatives. There she won five consecutive two-year terms, serving in the House from 1977 to 1987. She had run and lost for the U.S. Senate in 1974.

In 1986, she gave up her House seat to try for the Senate again and this time she was rewarded. She has won three terms, the last of which is due to expire on January 3, 2005. The history of women in the Senate stretches back to 1922, although the first female member of the political body was only appointed for two days.

Rebecca Latimer Felton of Georgia was appointed to fill a vacancy in 1992. At 87, the appointment capped off a long, successful career in politics for Felton.

The first women elected to the Senate was Hattie Wyatt Caraway of Arkansas. Caraway was originally appointed to the Senate to fill the vacancy resulting from the death of her husband, Thaddeus Caraway, in 1931. Mrs. Carraway then ran for reelection and won in 1932. Six years later, she was reelected and served in the Senate until 1945.

After the 1992 elections, the Senate had tripled its number of women to six. In addition to Moseley-Braun, two candidates from California were elected to make that the first state to have two female senators.

Dianne Feinstein had been the mayor of San Francisco from 1978 to 1988. She ran for governor of California in 1990, but lost the race. Two years later, she was elected as a Democrat to fill the term left vacant by the resignation of Pete Wilson. In the 1992 race, she received the most votes of any candidate who ever ran for the Senate.

She was joined in the Senate by Barbara Boxer. Boxer had been a U.S. Representative for five terms, serving in the House from 1983 to 1993. In 1992, she decided to run for the Senate and she won. Despite being the weaker of the two women candidates in the state, Boxer won reelection in 1998.

The fourth woman elected to the Senate in 1992 was Patty Murray, a Democrat from Washington. A former two-term member of her state Senate, she won both her 1992 race and her reelection six years later.

Before the 1992 elections, the Senate added another female when Jocelyn Burdick was named to fill out the vacancy left when her husband died. Burdick, a Democrat, was appointed in September of 1992 and only served until December of the same year. At that time, a special election was held to fill out the rest of the term of Quentin Northrop Burdick. Jocelyn Burdick did not run for reelection.

Not even a year after the 1992 elections, the Senate added another women, this time Republican Kay Bailey Hutchinson of Texas. The former Texas state treasurer won a special election in June 1993. She was elected to fill the term of Lloyd Bentsen, Jr. The next year, she was elected to a six-year term and in 2000, she won her second full term.

Moseley-Braun said she thought the increase of women in the Senate would "energize the process, bring a whole new set of skills to legislation to law making and policy making that I don't think have been as evident before now—like the ability to work in a bipartisan fashion when we have specific policy goals and the ability to work toward consensus.

"I hope to be a voice for people who might not otherwise be heard. I think that both Dianne [Feinstein, the Democratic Senator from California] and I bring a different kind of sensitivity to the kinds of issues that get raised in Judiciary."

The two new members on the Judiciary Committee faced a tough test right away. Newly elected President William J. Clinton nominated Zoe Baird for Attorney General. Then-general counsel of the Aetna Corporation, Baird would eventually withdraw her nomination after just one day of hearings when it was discovered that she and her husband had employed a Peruvian couple—a nanny and a chauffeur—who had no work papers.

After she withdrew, President Clinton named her to the President's Foreign Intelligence Advisory Board. In 1997, Baird was named the president of the John and Mary R. Markle Foundation, a New York-based philanthropic foundation.

The president's second choice for the post, Kimba Wood, also withdrew when it was discovered that she had hired an illegal immigrant as a babysitter. Wood argued that she was in compliance with the law, at the time, but admitted she had not disclosed this fact to the president's staff when she was being considered for the post.

The same type of problem cropped up for President Bush in 2003 when his choice for labor secretary came under scrutiny. Linda Chavez was criticized for allowing an illegal alien to live in her house.

AFRICAN AMERICANS WELCOMED IN WASHINGTON

While 1992 went down as the Year of the Woman, an alternate title might have been the year of the African American. Before the 1992 election, there were 25 African Americans in both parts of Congress. After the election, which was dominated by Clinton's win and other Democratic wins throughout the country, there were 39 African Americans in Congress.

Two of the new U.S. Representatives were African Americans, also from Illinois, Bobby Rush, and Mel Reynolds.

Four of the new minority representatives were women, Corinne Brown and Carrie Meek, both of Florida, Cynthia McKinney of Georgia, and Eva Clayton of North Carolina.

But shortly after the election, even bigger gains for African Americans were made at none other than 1600 Pennsylvania Avenue, the White House.

President Clinton picked six African Americans for his Cabinet. These choices made President Clinton's first Cabinet the most diverse Cabinet in history.

These included Ron Brown, the former Democratic National Committee chairman. Brown was chosen as Secretary of Commerce, the first African American to hold the post. Brown's tenure ended tragically, however, when he died in a plane crash in Croatia on April 3, 1996.

Jessie Brown, the former director of the Disabled Veterans of America, headed up the Veteran Affairs Department. Brown was a U.S. Marine veteran who suffered a partially paralyzed arm stemming from injuries he sustained during combat in Vietnam in 1965. Michael Espy, the first African-American representative from Mississippi since the Reconstruction, was chosen for Secretary of Agriculture. Just two years later, the Justice Department investigated charges that Espy received gifts from businesses regulated by his department. Before the investigation was closed, Espy announced his resignation, effective at the end of 1994.

Lee P. Brown, a former police chief in Atlanta, Houston, and New York City, was chosen to lead the Office of National Drug Control Policy. With drug use on the rise, and his budget decreasing, Brown resigned his post in December 1994.

Two minority women were added to the Cabinet, including Hazel R. O'Leary as Secretary of Energy and Dr. Joycelyn Elders as surgeon general. Elders was a talented physician known for her innovative research on diabetes, but her views on abortion rights and contraception in school health clinics made her a target for Republicans. Just two years after Clinton was elected, the Republicans gained a majority in Congress and were able to make life more difficult to some of Clinton's appointees.

Senator Moseley-Braun smiles during a press conference in 1995. Her status as the nation's first African-American female senator made her more high profile than most first-term senators.

The criticism of Elders heightened after she made remarks that implied that children should be taught about masturbation in sex education classes. Elders had actually said that when children were taught sex education in school, the class could include some information about masturbation.

One of Elders' biggest passions while in office was stemming the growing tide of people with AIDS. She felt that education of children, with a frank discussion about the implications of sex, would help achieve this goal.

●　　　●　　　●

Moseley-Braun's status as a nationally recognized African-American politician drew her into the debate on Elders. The White House asked her to support the surgeon general from Republican criticism. Moseley-Braun complied, called the debate about Elders statements "an inquisition," and the furor over her job "character assassination."

The senator's support could not stem the criticism of Elders in December 1994. After several stormy days, President Clinton asked for, and received Elders resignation.

But this issue showed the power that Moseley-Braun had garnered in such a short time. Her stamp as not only the first African-American senator, but also the only single, working mother in the Senate, made her a perfect spokeswoman for many issues. Because her historic win had given Moseley-Braun a high degree of name recognition across America, President Clinton didn't hesitate to ask for her help on many issues.

In return, her status rose much higher than the typical freshman senator. "She is a national celebrity," said Illinois State Senator Gary LaPaille. "It allows her to summon people to her office and get things faster than the normal U.S. senator from wherever. It allows her into meetings that other freshman senators wouldn't be invited to. And that's very good for Illinois."

"There's pressure to represent every group around," Moseley-Braun admitted. "Defining myself, as opposed to being defined by others, is one of the most difficult challenges I face."

For instance, when the ambitious national health plan was proposed by the president and First Lady Hillary Clinton, Moseley-Braun's reaction as to how the plan helped minorities was of national concerns. To make sure minorities were treated fairly, and to learn the complexities of the law, Moseley-Braun sat in on a handful of meetings with Mrs. Clinton as the law was prepared.

While part of her role was a burden, Moseley-Braun realized that the power from her position could also be used to push for ideas that she thought were important.

KEYING IN ON EDUCATION

It's no surprise that one of the main issues she dealt with in her 11 years as a state legislator, education, also became one of the key focuses of her term.

When asked by Farai Chideya, reporting for *Essence* magazine, to identify the one issue about which she felt most passionate, Moseley-Braun didn't hesitate to answer.

"Education, education, education. Education really will become the difference between the 'haves' and the 'have-nots' in the twenty-first century. Elementary and secondary education give children the opportunity to get literate, come out able to read, write and 'cipher,' as my grandmother used to say."

Moseley-Braun put together a complicated, wide-reaching education bill that sought to accomplish another first—getting the federal government to pay for its fair share of the costs of school renovations and building. She proposed a four-year, $5 billion bill to help assist states and municipalities in paying for new school buildings and renovations of older schools.

While the ability of local communities to control what they do in schools has long been revered in this country, Moseley-Braun said her bill would not take away any of a community's autonomy, but, rather, would provide some of the money necessary to get the needed work completed.

The U.S. General Accounting Office said in 1994, when Moseley-Braun pitched her bill, that 38 percent of the nation's urban schools were in such bad shape that they needed major renovations or total replacement. The same situations could be found at 30 percent of the country's rural schools and 29 percent of its suburban schools.

Moseley-Braun tried to garner support for her unconventional bill by comparing the nation's schools to the country's roads. Because a well-run system of roads betters not only the community the roads are based in, but also the country at large, the money to pay for these roads is split three ways: between the federal government, the state government, and the local community where the road is located. In these examples, however, the federal government carries most of the financial burden, up to 75 percent in many projects.

With regard to funding for education, however, Moseley-Braun pointed out that the federal government pays for about 7 percent of the nation's overall school costs. The bulk of the money for education spending in the nation actually comes from local property taxes.

If the country's roads were paid for this way, she says, the roads in rich areas would be well maintained, and the roads in poor areas would be in disrepair. That is the case in many of the schools in America today. Schools based in poor areas are typically in much worse shape than schools placed in well-heeled communities.

"Study after study has demonstrated a direct correlation between the conditions of school facilities and student achievement," Moseley-Braun said. "A disturbing number of our schools are literally crumbling around our students."

"I saw a school in southern Illinois that sent its students to the local prison for track practice, because the prison had

Thumbs up for education: Senator Moseley-Braun is seen here with son Matthew heading to the polls in November 1998. Moseley-Braun based her campaign for reelection on her education bill, on which she worked to gain President Clinton's support. She ultimately came up short, however, both on her proposed education bill and her bid for reelection.

better facilities," she told the *NEA Today*. "Some schools I visited are so crowded that stairway landings have been converted to computer labs, and study halls are literally being held in hallways."

Moseley-Braun's bill died because of a lack of support, including that of President Clinton who did not support it.

But she reworked the concept of the bill, to call for the federal government to offer $22 billion in interest-free bonds to school districts over two years. The cost to the government would have totaled about $3.3 billion over five years. This time, President Clinton got on board and supported her bill.

"It is estimated that the average cost of constructing a new maximum-security prison is more than $74,000 per prisoner. Estimates show the average cost of constructing a new school is less than $14,000 per student," she said. "We can clearly invest a little in schools to save a lot in jails."

Clinton mentioned the school facilities problems in two of his State of the Union addresses and he even included the money needed for the program in one of his budget requests to Congress.

While helping Moseley-Braun run for reelection, he spoke about how he changed his mind on this bill. "She persuaded me to offer a partial solution to a huge national challenge."

He continued, "Here's a case where she was out front on an issue. She said, 'We have a national interest.... We can't solve the whole problem, but we ought to give states and localities the incentive to do more.'"

Although her second plan garnered more support, Moseley-Braun ultimately came up short.

But there were areas in education where she did make a difference. During a 1998 speech for Moseley-Braun's reelection, President Clinton told a group in Chicago that the federal government provided the means to hire 100,000 new teachers to decrease the average class size to 18 in the early grades. "This is truly a historic accomplishment, the national government has never done anything like this before," he added.

Clinton also thanked Moseley-Braun for her support in helping to create a national reading program aimed at making sure all third graders can read and for supporting the funding to give schools money to hook up to the Internet.

Moseley-Braun also helped reinstate the student loan interest deduction. This law means that former students who are paying off student loans, can write off part of that loan on their income tax, saving them money and making it easier for more people to attend colleges.

Moseley-Braun also helped defeat a school voucher bill, a topic that is still being debated today. In 1997, a bill to allow children to use public school money to help pay for private school was proposed.

Moseley-Braun made her feelings on this issue clear. "Vouchers are about putting individuals over communities. The reason we have compulsory education in this country is not so that every child can access the best education his or her parents can find, but so that all our children can receive a quality education. If our public schools are not meeting that challenge, then it is our responsibility to fix them."

She also argued that the voucher system, which ultimately was defeated, would have drained money away from the very schools that need it the most.

RECOGNIZING THE UNDERGROUND RAILROAD

While education was Moseley-Braun's main focus during her term, she also sponsored a bill to commemorate sites on the Underground Railroad. The Underground Railroad was an informal network of homes owned by whites who were willing to hide black slaves as they made their way north. Although it's existence began during the colonial period, the number of slaves attempting to race to freedom reached its peak between 1830 and 1865.

The Fugitive Slave Act of 1850 made it illegal for anyone to help a slave make their way north to freedom. This resulted in the Underground Railroad members honing their ability to provide shelter to escaping slaves without their presence becoming common knowledge. Many homes along the path were built with small spaces where slaves could hide in case any town officials came to investigate.

The railroad helped thousands of slaves to freedom, including Harriet Tubman and Frederick Douglass, both of whom would later go on to become famous African Americans. Tubman, who escaped to freedom in 1849, returned to the South at least 15 times to rescue hundreds of other slaves.

Douglass, who escaped in 1847, began publishing the *North Star* newspaper in Rochester, New York.

The Underground Railroad existed in at least 34 states. A typical trip might be 560 miles. A healthy, strong slave might make this trip in two months, but for others, or those caught in bad weather, the journey could last an entire year.

The National Park Service, the group that oversaw documenting the sites, has named at least 38 places as being part of the Underground Railroad.

Moseley-Braun hailed the bravery of both whites and African Americans when she sought to pass the legislation. "The Underground Railroad bridged the divides of race, religion, sectional differences and nationality, spanned state lines and international borders and joined the American ideals of liberty and freedom expressed in the Declaration of Independence and the Constitution to the extraordinary actions of ordinary men and women working in common purpose to free people."

One of the sites commemorated in the act belonged to Richard Eells, a doctor in Quincy, Illinois. Eells was found guilty in 1842 for violating the Fugitive Slave Act. His case was tried by Stephen Douglas, who went on to become a U.S. senator and a leading figure in the debate over slavery.

In 1998, President Bill Clinton (seated) signed the Underground Railroad Act, a bill sponsored by Senator Carol Moseley-Braun. Applauding the President are Representative Louis Stokes (left), Secretary of Transportation Rodney Slater (right), Senator Mike DeWine (second from right), and Senator Moseley-Braun (center).

In the case, Eells was caught helping a slave, known only as Charley, escape out of Mississippi into Illinois. Eells' house sat right on the Mississippi River at the westernmost point of the state. Eells was fined $400, a hefty amount for 1842.

Moseley-Braun said that when she first joined the Senate, and the group held its first meeting in the Capitol's Old Senate Chamber, she felt the history in the room. The Senate met in that chamber from 1810 to 1859 and

Moseley-Braun made it a point to seek out the seat that Stephen Douglas sat in when he was in office.

"As I positioned myself in his place, I could not help becoming overwhelmed by the justice that the people of Illinois had finally given Charley and Dr. Eells.

"The legacy of the Underground Railroad is its affirmation of the triumph of the human spirit over America's original sin. It is almost impossible to imagine today how profoundly difficult and singularly unpopular the positions of Charley and Dr. Eells must have been in 1842.

"You have to be very motivated to cross the Mississippi River under the cover of darkness; you have to be fanatically committed to risk life and property to help a lawbreaker escape to freedom. And yet, all of the participants—the blacks and whites who together flouted racism and slavery's unjust legal framework—not only have provided us with a proud chapter in our history, but also have pointed the way to our future."

7

Mistakes and Criticisms

"We [Moseley-Braun and her campaign] spent four
years with a 100 percent audit with the Federal
Election Commission on 'campaign-finance
irregularities.' When it was all over, they said, 'Have
a nice day.' And yet, every time my name gets
mentioned in press reports, it's 'campaign-finance
irregularities.' I guess the notion is that you couldn't
handle $7 million and not steal some of it."
—Carol Moseley-Braun, Chideya, *Essence,* October 1998

Even before she was elected, it was obvious that Carol
Moseley-Braun would not be a typical senator. She
gained national attention after her primary win, secured
coveted exposure by speaking at the Democratic National
Convention, and fulfilled her campaign's promise by
becoming the first African-American woman elected to the
U.S. Senate.

Senator Moseley-Braun fields reporters'questions about her campaign finances at a news conference on Capitol Hill in 1996. A Federal Election Commission audit of her campaign finances revealed sloppy record keeping and improper contributions.

Moseley-Braun's notoriety didn't end there. Less than a year into her term, she took on, and beat, Senate veteran Jesse Helms. But all the attention Moseley-Braun garnered was not positive.

In April 1996, *Newsweek* reported that Moseley-Braun still had half a million dollars of debt stemming from her 1992 campaign. The magazine reported that an investigation into her campaign finances was slowed by the 42 amendments she filed to her campaign report. Aides said any investigation was also slowed when a power surge wiped a list of donors and expenses off a computer.

For the general campaign, Moseley-Braun's team raised more than $6 million. Of that, $1 million was spent on television advertising. When the race ended, the campaign was $544,000 in debt.

An unflattering feature story in the *New Republic's* Nov. 15, 1993 issue accused Moseley-Braun of conducting an extravagant campaign, including paying campaign manager Kgosie Matthews $15,000 a month, when the typical pay for that position is about $7,000.

CRITICISM FROM WITHIN

Even some of her supporters criticized Moseley-Braun. Kay Clement, her Hyde Park neighbor who encouraged her in 1978 to run for her first elected office as a state representative, quit Moseley-Braun's campaign shortly after the primary. "I kept hearing terrible things about how the money was being spent," Clement told the *New Republic.* "The campaign was conspicuous consumption. It turned into something resembling a rock 'n' roll tour."

The *New Republic* charged that the candidate and her campaign manager used the most luxurious accommodations when they traveled; that she moved into an expensive Chicago apartment after her win, that she paid cash for a new Jeep Cherokee and that she, Matthews and her son went on a 26-day vacation in South Africa after the win. The magazine said the three flew the Concorde for the trip; the superfast airplane cost about $4,000 per one-way ticket.

Campaign press secretary David Eichenbaum complained about Moseley-Braun to the *New Republic* as well. "All we knew was that a lot was being spent," he said. "It was shocking to some of us that two weeks before the election, when we had raised almost $7 million, the campaign had to borrow hundreds of thousands to be competitive on TV."

The Internal Revenue Service twice recommended that the Justice Department set up a grand jury to hear evidence against Moseley-Braun, but both times the agency was rebuffed.

The debate caused the Federal Election Commission to investigate claims that Moseley-Braun misused campaign contributions, but the commission never filed any charges against the Illinois senator.

In a 1998 interview with *Essence* magazine, Moseley-Braun addressed the question of financial impropriety.

"We spent four years with a 100 percent audit with the Federal Election Commission on 'campaign-finance irregularities.' When it was all over, they said, 'Have a nice day.' And yet, every time my name gets mentioned in press reports, it's 'campaign-finance irregularities.' I guess the notion is that you couldn't handle $7 million and not steal some of it."

Eichenbaum also criticized Moseley-Braun for ignoring position papers created by her staff. Instead of releasing the papers in July when she got them, they weren't released until late October, just weeks before the general election.

"The campaign sure didn't have a message beyond Carol's personality," Eichenbaum said. "Every day was an exercise in trying to give the candidate a message beyond just, 'Here I am, superstar.'"

Every session, senators cast hundreds of votes on issues that range from international affairs to the most mundane issues domestically. Although there were several times where Moseley-Braun's vote helped decide an issue in favor of President Clinton and the Democrats, one vote she took in 1995 resulted in heavy criticism.

In 1996, while a member of the Senate Finance Committee, Moseley-Braun voted to preserve a legal loophole that would end up giving drug giant Glaxo Wellcome an extra two years on its patent for Zantac. Zantac is a popular medicine used to treat ulcers. When a drug company has a patent on a particular drug, the company is the only one who can produce it, meaning they can control how much it costs.

Once the company loses its patent for the drug, the medicine can be produced generically by any company. This results in a lower price for basically the same drug.

Once the patent expires, the company also loses its exclusive ability to sell the drug. So not only does it have to lower the drug's price, but it inevitably ends up selling less of the drug than it did when it had patent control.

Her fellow senator from Illinois, Democrat Paul Simon, said Moseley-Braun's vote cost consumers millions of dollars that they could have saved by buying a generic version of the drug.

In the case of North Carolina's Glaxo, Moseley-Braun was criticized because of her relationship with the company's CEO and the amount of money the company gave Moseley-Braun.

Glaxo's CEO at the time of the vote was Robert Ingram. He and Moseley-Braun were friends from back in the days when she used to be in the state legislature. During those days, Ingram was a lobbyist.

Shortly after Moseley-Braun was elected, but before she was sworn in, Glaxo paid her $15,000 to speak. Because she was not yet a senator, this fee did not violate the Senate's limit on honorariums, which is the amount a senator can be paid for a political speech.

Glaxo's kindness didn't stop there. The company political action group and its executives contributed almost $17,000 to Moseley-Braun's reelection campaign, reported *Crain's Chicago Business*.

"There is rarely a vote you make that someone cannot stretch the cord and find a relationship," she said of the appearance that her vote was to help Glaxo. Ending the patent would have required the senate to make an amendment to 1994's General Agreement of Tariffs and Trades.

NIGERIAN TRIP BRINGS CRITICISM

One event that caused even her supporters to question her motives was Moseley-Braun's trip to Nigeria in 1996.

During her four-day trip abroad, Moseley-Braun met with the country's military ruler, Gen. Sani Abacha. According to a story in *Newsweek*'s August 26, 1996 issue, Abacha took power after a 1993 coup. Once in charge, the magazine said he jailed the country's elected president, imprisoned as many as 7,000 political opponents, and allegedly stole more than $1 billion in oil revenues.

The magazine said he also ordered the murder of nine environmental activists from the Ogoni tribe and of playwright Ken Saro-Wiwa.

Yet Moseley-Braun not only met with the dictator, but didn't meet any of the pro-democracy leaders who oppose Abacha. Matthews, Moseley-Braun's former campaign manager, was formerly a lobbyist for the Nigerian government.

Although Moseley-Braun aides told *Newsweek* that the senator did not characterize the regime "positively or negatively," she told a group of journalists in Abuja, "I think we have an obligation to see to it that our policy in Nigeria is formulated based on facts and not on fiction or prejudice."

"We expect that democratic forces should be on our side, to show sympathy and support," Abdul Oroh told *Newsweek*. Oroh is executive director of the Civil Liberties Organization, a Lagos-based human rights watchdog group. "When someone such as Moseley-Braun gets comfortable with a tyrannical, illegitimate government, we wonder what's going on. We wonder who are our friends."

Nigerian President General Sani Abacha salutes during a 1997 summit meeting of the Economic Community of West African States. Senator Moseley-Braun received strong criticism for meeting with General Abacha, who is accused of murdering his political opponents and stealing vast sums of money from Nigeria.

Jesse Jackson also opposed the trip.

The senator never told the State Department that she was taking this trip. The department later characterized the time as a "private trip."

The visit undercut an official government visit from Democratic U.S. Representative Bill Richardson of New Mexico. Richardson made his trip to press Abacha on his human rights record.

While Moseley-Braun said she maintained her neutrality during her visits, she opposed the Nigeria Democracy Act.

This would have slapped a number of sanctions on Nigeria, from halting U.S. investments to freezing the junta's assets. Moseley-Braun argued that imposing sanctions on Nigeria and not China, another country with a poor human rights record, would be a "double standard" that was racist.

When longtime *Newsweek* columnist George Will wrote a column in 1998 criticizing Moseley-Braun for her financial problems and her unauthorized trip to Nigeria, she fought back. "I think because he could not say 'nigger,' he said the word 'corrupt,'" she said on television. "George Will can just take his hood and go back to wherever he came from."

Will had not called Moseley-Braun corrupt and within hours of her statement, she apologized. The next day, she faxed an apology to Will.

In her October 1998 interview with *Essence* magazine, Moseley-Braun addressed some of the issues that lingered after her Nigerian trip.

When the magazine asked why she went, Moseley-Braun replied: "I have yet to find anybody who can explain to me why we should have one set of rules for Africa and another set of rules for the rest of the world.... There is nobody more committed to democracy and human rights and world affairs than I am.... But to say human rights means one thing in China, one thing in Mexico, one thing in Burma, but that there's another standard altogether for these Africans doesn't make sense to me."

She went on to say in the interview that when she met General Abacha she encouraged him on democracy, human rights issues and releasing all the political prisoners his government put in jail.

8

The Incumbent Falls

"The money was not there and that had a double impact. Not only wasn't I able to spend as much on media as my opponent, but the time I could have spent campaigning in other parts of the state I had to devote to fundraising."
—Carol Moseley-Braun, *Black Enterprise*

The federal government operates within a system of checks and balances. Congress makes laws, but needs approval from both the House of Representatives and the Senate to pass a bill to the president. The president can't write a law, but Congress has to seek approval to pass a law. If the president refuses, Congress can override the decision, but only if both groups garner support from 75 percent of its members.

The Supreme Court, the highest court in the country, interprets laws. While the president and Congress can't reverse any Supreme Court action, the president gets to make

Putting on her game face: Senator Moseley-Braun smiles as she listens to a caller's question during a 1997 radio interview. Bombarded by questions about her campaign finances and her meeting with Nigerian President General Sani Abacha, she faced an uphill battle for reelection that year.

nominations for new Supreme Court members. Then the Senate has to confirm the nomination. These confirmations are lifetime.

In much the same way as these three parts of government work together, so does the framework of elected politicians in Washington, D.C. The president is elected every four years, the members of the House of Representatives are elected every two years, and senators are elected for the longest term of all, six years.

The different length terms for all three groups can be important. For instance, when Bill Clinton won the presidency for the first time in 1992, many other Democrats won office, in part helped by his drawing power at the top of the party ticket. Moseley-Braun was one of the first-time national winners helped by Clinton's victory over President George H. W. Bush in 1992.

But just two years later, Republicans surged forward at the polls, regaining majority control of both houses in Congress.

Two years after that, in 1996, the pendulum swung back to Democrats again, as President Clinton easily won a second term.

In 1998, the year that Moseley-Braun and two other prominent liberal Democratic senators were up for reelection, the country had turned against the president. After his 1996 reelection, President Clinton faced questions that he skirted campaign laws while fundraising.

In 1997, Paula Jones sued Clinton for sexual harassment based on an event that she said took place when Clinton was still governor of Arkansas. It was during the proceedings of this suit that the incident that Clinton would become best known for erupted.

Government employee Linda Tripp told independent counsel Kenneth Starr that she had proof that the president asked someone in the trial to lie.

In January 1998, Tripp came forward with audiotapes she had made from conversations with Monica Lewinsky. She said the tape proved that Clinton wanted Lewinsky to lie under oath about their affair. Clinton later admitted to having a relationship with Lewinsky, then a White House intern.

The details about Clinton's relationship with Lewinsky spilled out over a year's time, as both the president and the intern were called to testify in the case.

As the trial ended, the House of Representatives impeached Clinton, making him only the second president ever impeached. Later, the Senate had a chance to convict the president on charges that he committed perjury and obstruction of justice in the case. For the president to be found guilty, three-quarters of the Senate had to agree to the charges. In the end, neither vote won even a simply majority.

Clinton's presidency was saved, but many of the accomplishments he had gathered in his first six years were obscured. Because liberal politicians, such as Moseley-Braun, were always closely tied to Clinton, it was important for her and her followers to try to point out the president's accomplishments.

In the three presidential elections before 1992, the Democratic nominee averaged just more than 58 electoral votes, a scant 11 percent of the electoral votes available. But in two races, Clinton averaged 375 electoral votes. He never won more than 50 percent of the vote, but part of that was due to the persistent third-party campaign of billionaire Ross Perot. Clinton did garner 49 percent of the popular vote in 1996.

As a legislator, he produced the first balanced budget in 30 years, saw 22 million jobs created during his eight years in office, saw unemployment rates drop to their lowest point in 30 years, and presided over the longest economic expansion in American history.

During Clinton's eight years as president, the country's crime rate hit its lowest level in 26 years, the nation added 100,000 police officers, reduced the welfare payroll to its lowest state in 32 years and the poverty rate to its lowest level in 20 years.

FINDING ACT TWO DIFFICULT

Everyone knew that Moseley-Braun would face a tough reelection battle in Illinois in 1998. Even when she won the 1992 election, 56 percent of the voters said they didn't trust her. That was because of the scandals she had to face during her campaign. These included withholding some of her mother's money from Medicaid to running up a $544,000 debt in the campaign to backing her campaign manager against sexual harassment charges.

As a liberal Democrat, she was also tied closely to President Clinton. Moseley-Braun benefited from Clinton's appeal in 1992, but his personal troubles hurt her in 1998.

"She had been looking vulnerable for a long time," said David Bositis, a political analyst with the Joint Center for Political and Economic Studies. "She was elected in 1992. Two years later, the Republicans took over the Senate and suddenly she was a black female junior member of the Senate whose party was in the minority. It's a recipe for being ineffective."

Part of the problem may have been all the praise Moseley-Braun garnered with her historic 1992 win. "She was a symbol when she was elected, both as an accomplished African-American politician and an accomplished female politician," said Mark Hansen, professor of political science at the University of Chicago. "And I think it's hard for a real human being to measure up to a symbol," he told the *Los Angeles Times*.

In the same article, Kenneth Janga, a professor of political science at Northwestern University, said: "She got elected on personal characteristics, and it appears she [could] lose it on personal characteristics.... We attributed a lot of qualities to her that she didn't really have—mainly political acumen. She just did a lot of really dumb things."

Moseley-Braun's opponent was state Senator Peter Fitzgerald. He was a 38-year-old multimillionaire who was as conservative as Moseley-Braun was liberal.

Fitzgerald's family had amassed a fortune in the banking industry and he wasn't afraid to use some of it during his election. Moseley-Braun raised about $8 million for her reelection, but she estimated that Fitzgerald spent twice that amount.

"The money was not there and that had a double impact," Moseley-Braun said. "Not only wasn't I able to spend as much on media as my opponent, but the time I could have spent campaigning in other parts of the state I had to devote to fundraising," she told *Black Enterprise* magazine.

Fitzgerald ran his campaign by staying out of the spotlight and letting the race hinge on Moseley-Braun and what the public thought of her accomplishments and her mistakes.

In a way, the race echoed the split the nation felt about President Clinton. People had to balance his private life versus the accomplishments he had politically.

Two of the other women who first won election to the Senate in 1992 were also having trouble getting reelected.

Patty Murray was the liberal Democrat who ran in the state of Washington, as a "mom in tennis shoes." Although her win was part of the Year of the Woman, she battled lackluster job ratings in her six years. Like Moseley-Braun, she faced a conservative Republican, state representative Linda Smith. Smith had never lost a race, and boosted a 35,000-person volunteer army. But

Moseley-Braun wipes away tears as she speaks at a news conference on November 4, 1998, just hours after conceding the U.S. Senate race to challenger Peter Fitzgerald.

despite the race being close, Murray was able to retain her seat.

Barbara Boxer of California also was hurt by her close affiliation with President Clinton. "This campaign in many ways is a very surreal campaign. Nobody, or almost nobody, is focusing on the issues ... so I've got to do it myself," Boxer told the Associated Press. Boxer was running neck-and-neck with Republican state treasurer Matt Fong. Eventually, she bested Fong and won re-election.

Moseley-Braun's supporters tried to turn the focus back on her accomplishments.

"The real issues are what she is doing for black women, what she is doing for single women, what she is doing for families. Those are the only things that matter," said Portland Reed, a law school graduate who attended one of Moseley-Braun's Chicago rallies.

"I think if she loses, we as a nation will lose an extremely important voice in American politics," said Hilary Shelton, acting director of the Washington chapter of the National Association for the Advancement of Colored People. "Diversity of thought has always been seen as part of the genius of our political system. But the Senate has always fallen behind in that diversity."

Fitzgerald disagreed, telling the *Los Angeles Times*, "The most important qualification for a U.S. senator is that people be able to have faith in the ethics and judgment of their U.S. senator. I think she is vulnerable on questions of ethics and judgment."

On another occasion, Fitzgerald said, "She has a pattern of helping out specific businesses," referring specifically to Moseley-Braun's Glaxo vote. "I would be more reliable on business issues."

Tired of the constant criticism, Moseley-Braun blamed the media, telling the *Los Angeles Times* that bad treatment by the media had hurt her unnecessarily. "If I had a bigger press staff, I might have a different image," she said.

These statements about Moseley-Braun from supporters show how far she had fallen in her six-year term.

Hillary Rodham Clinton, then the First Lady, said, "I'm giving Carol another chance."

A Democrat state legislator told the *Los Angeles Times*, "I'm feeling [her campaign] turning around."

Even the candidate herself admitted that she was getting "over the hump."

When the election arrived, the race was close and so were the results. Fitzgerald took 51 percent of the vote, and Moseley-Braun was no longer a U.S. senator.

"If one body of our political institution now has no blacks participating, what does that say," asked Ron Walters, a political scientist at the University of Maryland. "There's no substitute for the blacks being able to represent themselves as part of our mosaic. And our absence continues to say we're not yet whole. She was a point person for issues having to deal with the black agenda and she carried many from the Congressional Black Caucus into the Senate."

STARTING HER LIFE AFTER

Immediately after her loss, Moseley-Braun started planning for the rest of her life. Even before her term expired, President Clinton appointed her as a consultant for the Department of Education. The job paid her about $450 a day; as a senator, she had been making $125,000 a year.

Her contract called on Moseley-Braun to provide expertise on school construction issues, a topic close to her heart. But because her several attempts to have the federal government pay for school construction failed, the Department of Education had no budget for building items.

Shortly after this, the president nominated Moseley-Braun to be ambassador to New Zealand.

Moseley-Braun's political career was sparked by her reaction to the Clarence Thomas nomination hearing in the Senate, and now she would face the same process. Former senators are routinely accepted for these slots, but there was one complicating factor. The person in charge of the Senate committee was none other than Jesse Helms.

Six years after she had bested him in the very public issue regarding the Daughters of the Confederacy, Moseley-Braun was going to have to get Helms' approval for her new post.

Helms did not immediately openly criticize her nomination, but he did not act on it either. As the chairman of the Senate Foreign Relations Committee, he just refused to bring the matter up for debate.

At one point he said, "I don't think she should hold her breath until she becomes an ambassador. She should look for another line of work."

He admitted that he still had bitter feelings about the 1993 vote that he lost because of Moseley-Braun's impassioned speech.

Helms told *Roll Call*, a Capitol Hill newspaper, "At the very minimum, she has got to apologize for the display that she provoked over a little symbol for a wonderful group of little old ladies."

In a statement Helms office released, he criticized President Clinton for the nomination. "This nomination comes to the Senate with an ethical cloud hanging over Ms. Moseley-Braun. Indeed, I wonder if the president and his associates even examined her record before submitting it to the Senate."

The president answered back, as quoted by the *Los Angeles Times*. "There has been an unprecedented amount of playing politics with ambassadors," he said. The Senate is delaying "four other ambassadors that no one has questioned anything about their qualifications, for a totally irrelevant reason."

After about one month, in November 1999, Helms relented when he got the White House to turn over thousands of pages of documents about Moseley-Braun. Helms did not attend the committee meeting that allowed the entire Senate to vote on Moseley-Braun's ambassadorship.

The Senate voted 96–2 to confirm the Chicago Democrat. The only negative votes were Helms and Republican Peter Fitzgerald, who defeated Moseley-Braun just a year earlier.

In a way, Moseley-Braun was lucky the White House got Helms to relent. After her delay, Helms blocked the appointment of former Massachusetts governor William Weld as ambassador to Mexico. Weld criticized Helms's stalling tactics. Helms never brought Weld's name up for a vote on his committee and Weld eventually withdrew his name.

Helms's tricks continued even when President George W. Bush won in 2000. Helms delayed votes on several top Treasury officials to force concessions from Bush on textile imports.

In 2001, Moseley-Braun became a professor of politics at Morris Brown College in Atlanta. She taught a course in government at the historically black college.

"I'm excited to be in the classroom teaching young people about government, because if you like politics, you have to understand government," she told *Jet*.

"I don't presume to come in knowing how to be a professor, but I know my subject matter cold."

At the same time, Moseley-Braun became a consultant with Andrew Young at GoodWorks International.

"They have created a market to support and assist U.S. businesses in their endeavors in the second- and third-worlds," Moseley-Braun told the *Atlanta Journal-Constitution*. "My experience in the Senate and as an ambassador brings another piece to the worldwide focus they have here."

9

Going for the White House

"Now I am prepared to breach the last barrier, shatter the last great glass ceiling that limits the contributions a woman can make in the leadership of this country. New Zealand, where I served as ambassador, has had two women prime ministers. America is ready for its first woman president. My campaign will be a people's campaign. We will listen to every-day people, we will register voters, we will mobilize those who perhaps have questioned the relevance of this process."
—Carol Moseley-Braun, *Carol Moseley-Braun Web Site*
(www.carolforpresident.com)

After her 1998 loss, Moseley-Braun was quick to say that she wasn't running for office again. It appeared to be an easy choice, given the controversies that dogged her and were sure to pop up again if she ran.

It seemed that her political career was over, and although her time in the national spotlight was brief, Moseley-Braun

Ms. President? Former Senator Moseley-Braun announces her plans to form an exploratory committee for a Democratic presidential bid during a 2003 press conference. If elected, Moseley-Braun would be the first female president of the United States and the first minority president.

had certainly made her mark. Her obvious high mark was her Senate win, but along the way she had distinguished herself as a tireless advocate for education and civil rights.

Moseley-Braun seemed to have settled into her life as both a professor and consultant with GoodWorks. But politics is in her blood, and as numerous Democrats considered running for the Democratic presidential nomination in 2004, Moseley-Braun's name began to surface.

One of the first Democrats to announce his candidacy was the Rev. Al Sharpton, a New York clergyman who has long been in the news for fighting civil rights battles, but had never sought public office before. Because Sharpton was the first African American to declare, many in the party seemed worried that he would generate an undue amount of support from African Americans. This group is a vital part of the Democrat's chance for success on a national level.

Although no one was predicting that Sharpton would ever win the nomination, or even come close, some in the party were worried that if he became too powerful he might be able to demand the eventual nominee to make changes to his or her views that would hurt the candidate in the general election.

When Democratic leaders looked around for another strong African-American candidate, they immediately thought of Moseley-Braun, who in 2002 had turned 55 years old.

In October of 2002, she admitted that she was thinking of listening to their overtures. "My supporters are encouraging me to advance to public office again," she told the *BET.com* staff. "Which office depends on where I can be the most service to the people. It could be as easy for the Senate or the mayorship or the presidency, frankly," she added.

"There is no reason that there cannot be a confluence of elements and of issues and of time and of events, so this would be a good time for her," said Yvonne Scruggs-Leftwich, a friend of Moseley-Braun's.

A few months later, in January 2003, Moseley-Braun told Democratic Party Chairman Terry McAuliffe that she was ruling out another bid for the Senate so she could consider the highest office in the country, the presidency.

"To have a prominent African-American female out there making the case for the party would be great," said McAuliffe. "The more candidates the better."

"The Democratic Party is running on the same tank of gas we had in 1992," Donna Brazile told Knight-Ridder and the Tribune News Service. Brazile was the former manager of Vice President Al Gore's presidential bid in 2000.

"I don't find it a ridiculous notion," said Minyon Moore, to Knight Ridder. Minyon, the former chief operating officer at the Democratic National Committee, said she has talked with Moseley-Braun about her possible run. "When people are being fair to Carol, they know how smart she is."

At least one political observer seemed to think that Moseley-Braun would have a tough time shedding herself of the former charges she faced. "Obviously, Richard Nixon tells us that it is possible to have a second act in politics," said Kent Redfield, a professor of political science at the University of Illinois at Springfield. "She came in as the first African-American woman elected to the Senate, but the prevailing opinion was that she had really squandered all of the advantages and all of the opportunities."

Brazile said she could learn from her past mistakes. "She was new to the game. When you don't understand the rules, you don't know how to play."

One friend of Moseley-Braun's cautioned that it would be a mistake to discount her if she decided to run. "When Bill Clinton first started, no one thought he would do well. No one gave Jimmy Carter a chance," said Denver Mayor Wellington Webb. Webb, who was born in Chicago, added, "You don't deprive anyone the opportunity to run. The more who want to run, the more energy it creates for our party."

A month later, in February 2003, Moseley-Braun laid out what she expected to be the arc of her campaign if she decided to run for president. "If the American people respond to my message and respond to my candidacy, then it will be a viable one.... If they don't, then we'll probably fold our tent in September or thereabouts and support whoever the Democratic nominee might be. But I have every intention of winning the nomination."

The race is impossible to call months before the party has to start to winnow the field down to one candidate.

Beside Moseley-Braun and Sharpton, the Democrats who have already announced that they will run include Massachusetts Senator John Kerry, Vermont Governor Howard Dean, North Carolina Senator John Edwards, Missouri U.S. Representative Dick Gephardt, and Connecticut Senator and former vice presidential candidate Joe Lieberman. Others thought to be interested in running include Florida Senator Bob Graham, former Colorado Senator Gary Hart, and Connecticut's second Senator Christopher Dodd.

Lieberman and Gephardt were the early leaders in a poll of likely Democratic voters. Lieberman had garnered 16 percent of people's support in the poll, while Gephardt had 13 percent. Moseley-Braun was in the middle of the pack with 4 percent of support.

Finally, Moseley-Braun made the decision she had been edging toward—the person who was the first female African-American senator was going to attempt two more firsts, the first minority to become president and the first woman to become president.

When Moseley-Braun announced her candidacy, the nation was debating whether or not the country would go to war to oust Iraq leader Saddam Hussein and eliminate what leaders expected were weapons of mass destruction.

Moseley-Braun quickly stated her position on this key issue. "I believe we should not go to war unilaterally and I'm very clear that we should not have budget deficits," she said, criticizing current President George W. Bush.

The former senator reacted angrily to questions that she was only in the race to offset Sharpton's popularity. "I am going to be competing for everybody's vote who participates in a Democratic primary," she told the Associated Press.

She also waved off the suggestion that both her gender and her race will make it impossible for her to eventually win. "I have never believed that I should be limited by gender or race. When I was a little girl, I wanted to go out and have adventures and that's what I'm doing."

Beyond defending herself, Moseley-Braun went on to tout her qualifications. "On paper, I'm the most credentialed candidate in the race," she said. "I'm the only candidate that has international experience as an ambassador. I served in the United States Senate and that puts me in the same zone as some of the other [candidates]."

One old friend, Peg Breslin, agrees. Breslin is a former appellate judge and state representative. She said that Moseley-Braun's themes of fighting the root cause of terrorism, cutting the national debt and improving health care and schools could earn her a good audience. "If she is diligent enough and has some good handlers and gets some good breaks, she is capable of commanding the issues," Breslin said.

Speaking before the National Press Club in Washington, D.C., Moseley-Braun said: "Duct tape is not a substitute for diplomacy. And I believe the people can

Presidential candidate Carol Moseley-Braun is surrounded by supporters at a 2003 meeting at the University of Chicago Law School. The former senator announced that her campaign slogan is "It's time to take the 'Men Only' sign off the White House door."

and must demand an end to the saber rattling that has made us all a hostage to fear."

She said she would campaign for women voters; her slogan is: "It's time to take the 'Men Only' sign off the White House door."

Brazile said that to gain momentum, Moseley-Braun has to raise her profile to all voters, raise money and band together a broad group of advisors. With many of the Democratic primaries moved up, the candidate can be solidified by February 2004. That's a month before Illinois will have its primary, where Moseley-Braun could expect a strong showing.

In an interview with *USA Today* columnist DeWayne Wickham, Moseley-Braun clarified some of her stances on national issues. "I'm a fiscal hawk and a peace dove. War with Iraq will not solve our domestic-security needs, will not defeat terrorism and will not dry up the sources from which terrorism flows. And the tax cut, without regard to the cost of this war, is going to give us a $300 billion budget deficit. I think it's outrageous to give tax relief today that we're going to ask our grandchildren to pay for.

"I believe that Americans are prepared to go outside the box and elect a person who is female and African American, a person who does not fit the mold that we have resorted to for the last 200 years," Moseley-Braun told the columnist.

The presidential candidate expanded on her views during a television interview with PBS reporter Ray Suarez. Asked before the Iraq war about Iraq and its leader Saddam Hussein, she said: "I want to be a voice of hope for people who believe that we are clever enough to defeat terror without sacrificing our liberty. That we are creative enough to provide for peace and prosperity and progress in our time. And that we can come together as Americans to face the challenges of our time. And I believe that this administration is on the absolute wrong track, particularly in regard to using the war on terror as a subterfuge, as a cloak, if you will, for what is really an extreme political agenda."

Later on, she continued: "I hope to use this presidential campaign as an opportunity to talk about whether or not we think it's a good thing to cut teacher training and technology and education and health care for poor people, and healthcare for seniors."

"Iraq is not the only place where inspections need to happen. We are also threatened by other unstable states with nuclear and/or weapons of mass destruction capacity. So we will need the United Nations to help us deal with the threat from North Korea, for example. We will need the United Nations to help work out a resolution with regard to the whole standoff between India and Pakistan. There are a number of places around the world, not to mention coming to some kind of stability that provides for peace in the Middle East, I think those things are still possible."

Talking about issues outside Iraq and possible war, Moseley-Braun looked to her budget concerns. In a statement on her Web site, Carolforpresident.com, she wrote: "Our economy is in the doldrums of recession, retrenchment and reversal, not because of any natural phenomenon, or even the threat of war, but because of failed leadership.

"Budget deficits matter, and we have not the right to borrow from our children to pay for tax rebates today."

She finished the statement by explaining why she's running for president, but also giving a neat summarization of her career and all the key issues she's fought for in all her years in public office.

"Now I am prepared to breach the last barrier, shatter the last great glass ceiling that limits the contributions a woman can make in the leadership of this country. New Zealand, where I served as ambassador, has had two women prime ministers. America is ready for its first woman president. My campaign will be a people's campaign. We will listen to everyday people, we will register voters, we will mobilize those who perhaps have questioned the relevance of this process. . . .

"Ours is the greatest nation in the world not because we have the biggest military or the most money. America's greatness lies in the spirit of her people. That spirit of hope defines and undergirds the American Dream. Now is the time for Democrats to renew hope that we will leave that dream for the next generation in even better shape than we found it. And a woman can lead the way."

1947 Born Carol Moseley in Chicago on August 16.

1969 Receives her Bachelor of Arts degree from the University of Illinois.

1972 Receives her law degree from the University of Chicago.

1973 Joins the U.S. State's Attorney office in Chicago as an assistant U.S. attorney.

1978 Elected to the Illinois state legislator as a state representative.

1988 Becomes the Cook County Recorder of Deeds.

1992 Beats incumbent U.S. Senator Al Dixon in a three-way primary race; wins election to the U.S. Senate; is the first African-American woman to serve in the Senate.

1993 Takes office; uses impassioned speech about race to turn back an effort by fellow Senator Jesse Helms to approve a logo containing the Confederate flag.

1998 Loses reelection bid by 2 percentage points to Peter Fitzgerald; appointed U.S. Ambassador to New Zealand.

2001 Becomes a professor of politics at Morris Brown College in Atlanta.

2003 Decides to run for president of the United States.

Bibliography

African-Americans and Politics: The 1990s. U·X·L Multicultural, Gale Group, 1998.

Agron, Joe. "A National Agenda." *American School & University*, June 1994, p. 28.

Baum, Geraldine. "A Shock to the System." *Los Angeles Times*, March 17, 1992, p. 1.

Butler, John. "Carol Moseley-Braun's day to talk about race: a study of forum in the United States Senate." *Argumentation and Advocacy*, Fall 1995, p. 62.

Carol Moseley-Braun. DISCovery Biography, Gale Research, 1997.

Carol Moseley-Braun. U·X·L Biographies, Gale Group, 1999.

"Carol Moseley-Braun, Her First Year in Office." *Glamour*, Nov. 1993, *Current Biography*, June 1994.

"Carol Moseley-Braun." *Newsmakers*, 1993, Issue 4, Gale Research, 1993.

Chapman, Steve. "Chicago Hopeless." *New Republic*, Oct. 19, 1998, p. 19.

Chideya, Farai. "A Conversation with Senator Carol Moseley-Braun." *Essence*, Oct. 1998, p. 90.

"Diversity Wins." *Minneapolis Star Tribune*, Nov. 5, 1992.

"Fears and Expectations." *Economist*, Oct. 24, 1992, p. A25.

Gibbs, Nancy. "An Ugly Circus." *Time*, Oct. 21, 1991, p. 34.

McCormick, John, and Daniel Klaidman. "The Trials and Troubles of a Symbolic Senator." *Newsweek*, April 8, 1996.

Moseley-Braun, Carol. "Between W.E.B. Du Bois and B.T. Washington." *Ebony*, Nov. 1995, p. 58.

Nelson, Jill. "Carol Moseley-Braun: Power Beneath Her Wings." *Essence*, Oct. 1992, p. 56.

"Raw racism gets a black eye in the Senate." *National Catholic Reporter*, Aug. 13, 1993, p. 28.

"Sen. Carol Moseley-Braun Gets Committee OK for Bill to Highlight U.S. Underground Railroad Sites." *Jet*, June 8, 1998, p. 26.

Shalit, Ruth. "A Star is Born: the Old-New Politics of Moseley-Braun." *New Republic*, Nov. 15, 1993, p.18.

Smith, Eric L. "Changing of the Guard." *Black Enterprise*, January 1999, p. 17.

Smolowe, Jill. "She Said, He Said." *Time*, Oct. 21, 1991, p. 36.

"Tainted Victory." *Maclean's*, Oct. 28, 1991.

Time, Madigan. "Nine years later, Anita Hill is at peace, but she won't forget." *Knight-Ridder/Tribune News Service*, Nov. 21, 2000.

Weisberger, Bernard A. "A Quartet to Remember (African-American Senators)." *American Heritage*, April 1999, p. 16.

Wickham, DeWayne. "Black, female: Both impair Moseley-Braun's chances." *USA Today*, Feb. 24, 2003.

Wiesburg, Jacob. "Carol Moseley-Braun Making the Senate Floor a Focus for Matters of the Conscience." *Los Angeles Times*, Oct. 31, 1993, p. 3.

http://www.dems.us/moseley-braun/

http://www.carolforpresident.com/

http://www.senate.gov/

Further Reading

Agron, Joe. "A National Agenda." *American School & University*, June 1994, p. 28.

Butler, John. "Carol Moseley-Braun's day to talk about race: a study of forum in the United States Senate." *Argumentation and Advocacy*, Fall 1995, p. 62.

Carol Moseley-Braun. DISCovery Biography, Gale Research, 1997.

Carol Moseley-Braun. U*X*L Biographies, Gale Group, 1999.

"Carol Moseley-Braun." *Newsmakers*, 1993, Issue 4, Gale Research, 1993.

"Carol Moseley-Braun, Her First Year in Office." *Glamour*, Nov. 1993.

Chapman, Steve. "Chicago Hopeless." *New Republic*, Oct. 19, 1998, p. 19.

Chideya, Farai. "A Conversation with Senator Carol Moseley-Braun." *Essence*, Oct. 1998, p. 90.

"Fears and Expectations." *Economist*, Oct. 24, 1992, p. A25.

Gibbs, Nancy. "An Ugly Circus." *Time*, Oct. 21, 1991, p. 34.

McCormick, John, and Daniel Klaidman. "The Trials and Troubles of a Symbolic Senator." *Newsweek*, April 8, 1996. Current Biography, June 1994.

Nelson, Jill. "Carol Moseley-Braun: Power Beneath Her Wings." *Essence*, Oct. 1992, p. 56.

"Raw racism gets a black eye in the Senate." *National Catholic Reporter*, Aug. 13, 1993, p. 28.

Shalit, Ruth. "A Star is Born: the Old-New Politics of Moseley-Braun." *New Republic*, Nov. 15, 1993, p.18.

Smith, Eric L. "Changing of the Guard." *Black Enterprise*, January 1999, p. 17.

Wickham, DeWayne. "Black, female: Both impair Moseley-Braun's chances." *USA Today*, Feb. 24, 2003.

Wiesberg, Jacob. "Carol Moseley-Braun Making the Senate Floor a Focus for Matters of the Conscience." *Los Angeles Times*, Oct. 31, 1993, p. 3.

http://www.dems.us/moseley-braun/

http://www.carolforpresident.com/

http://www.senate.gov/

Index

Abacha, Sani
  Nigerian ruler, 77–78, 81
African Americans 8
  first female senator, 9, 42,
  44–45, 62–63, 72, 84, 96
  great leaders, 16–21, 28–29, 69
  in the U.S. Senate, 36–40,
  44–45, 51, 53, 102
  in Washington, D.C., 60–64, 88,
  94–96, 99
Alcorn College
  first college for blacks, 38
Alcorn, James L., 38
American Civil War, 38
Atlanta Journal-Constitution, 9
Axelrod, David
  on Moseley-Braun, 14, 41

Baird, Zoe
  appointments of, 59–60
Bennett, Robert (Senator), 53
Bentsen, Lloyd, Jr. (Senator), 59
Biden, Joseph (Senator), 49
Black Enterprise, 85
Black Reconstruction (Du Bois)
  contributions of blacks in, 19
Bositis, David, 84
Boston Globe, 42
Boxer, Barbara (Senator)
  Senate race of, 15, 58, 86–87
Bradley, Bill (Senator), 52
Braun, Matthew (son), 25, 66
Braun, Michael (husband), 25
Brazile, Donna
  on 2004 presidential race, 95, 98
Breslin, Peg
  on Moseley-Braun, 97
Brooke, Edward W.
  and civil rights, 40
  as Massachusetts' attorney
  general, 39

and the Senate, 39–40
Brown v. *Board of Education of Topeka*
  turning point in Civil Rights, 22
  and segregation of schools, 22
Brown, Corinne (Representative), 60
Brown, Jessie
  and the Veteran Affairs
  Department, 61
Brown, Lee P.
  as Officer of National Drug
  Control Policy, 61
Brown, Oliver, 22
Brown, Ron
  as Secretary of Commerce, 61
Bruce, Blanche K.
  achievements of, 39
  and the Senate, 37–39
Bryant, Roy
  and the murder of Till, 23–24
Burdick, Jocelyn (Senator)
  and the Senate, 58–58
Burdick, Quentin Northrop
  (Senator), 59
Bush, George H., 34
  and Thomas, 10, 30, 82
Bush, George W.
  appointments of, 60, 90
  criticism of, 97
Byrd, Robert (Senator), 54
Byrne, Jane (Mayor), 28

Campbell, Ben Nighthorse
  (Senator), 52
Caraway, Hattie Wyatt
  and the Senate, 58
Caraway, Thaddeus
  and the Senate, 58
Carter, Jimmy, 95
Chafee, John (Senator), 53
Chavez, Linda
  appointment of, 60

Index

Index

Index

death of, 28
  race for Illinois state
  representative, 26
Washington Post, 51
Webb, Wellington, 95
Weld, William
  appointment of, 90
Wenner, Jan
  support for Moseley-Braun, 13, 40
Wickham, DeWayne, 99

Williamson, Richard
  and the Senate race, 13–15, 40–44
Wilson, Pete (Senator), 58
Wood, Kimba
  appointment of, 60

Year of the Woman (1992), 14, 42,
  56, 60, 85
Young, Andrew, 90
Yourell, Harry, 29

Picture Credits

About the Author

Wayne D'Orio is a seasoned journalist who has worked for the *New York Times*, the *Hartford Courant*, and a host of other daily newspapers. The Rutgers University graduate lives in Connecticut, and currently works as editorial director of *District Administration*, a trade magazine that covers K–12 education for school superintendents.

South Campus
White Bear Lake Area High School
3551 McKnight Road
White Bear Lake, MN 55110